P9-CEM-296

PRONUNCIATION *plus* — PRACTICE THROUGH INTERACTION

MARTIN HEWINGS

SHARON GOLDSTEIN

WITHDRAWN

NORTH AMERICAN ENGLISH

CAMBRIDGE
UNIVERSITY PRESS

PUBLISHED BY THE PRESS SYNDICATE OF THE UNIVERSITY OF CAMBRIDGE
The Pitt Building, Trumpington Street, Cambridge, United Kingdom

CAMBRIDGE UNIVERSITY PRESS
The Edinburgh Building, Cambridge CB2 2RU, UK
40 West 20th Street, New York, NY 10011–4211, USA
477 Williamstown Road, Port Melbourne, VIC 3207, Australia
Ruiz de Alarcón 13, 28014 Madrid, Spain
Dock House, The Waterfront, Cape Town 8001, South Africa

http://www.cambridge.org

First published 1998
4th printing 2002

Printed in the United States of America

Typeset in New Aster and Frutiger

Library of Congress Cataloging-in-Publication Data
Hewings, Martin.
Pronunciation plus : practice through interaction : student's book
Martin Hewings, Sharon Goldstein.
p. cm.
ISBN 0-521-57797-7 (pb)
1. English language – Pronunciation by foreign speakers – Problems,
exercises, etc. 2. English language – Textbooks for foreign speakers.
I. Goldstein, Sharon. II. Title.
PE1137.H44 1998
428.3′4 – dc21   98-3653
                                                                                   CIP

A catalogue record for this book is available from the British Library

ISBN 0 521 57797 7 Student's Book
ISBN 0 521 57795 0 Cassettes
ISBN 0 521 57796 9 Teacher's Manual

Book design, page makeup and text composition: Leon Bolognese & Associates

Illustrations: Keith Bendis, Daisy de Puthod, Wally Neibart, Kevin Spaulding, Suffolk
Technical Illustrators, Andrew Toos

Contents

Key to phonetic symbols

Vowels			Consonants	
Symbol	**Examples**		**Symbols**	**Examples**
/ɑ/	stop, father		/b/	back, about
/æ/	apple, hat		/d/	dance, need
/aw/	out, town		/dʒ/	job, age
/ay/	ice, drive		/ð/	this, other
/ɛ/	end, red		/f/	four, off
/ey/	train, say		/g/	give, big
/ɪ/	if, big		/h/	hat, behind
/iy/	jeans, see		/k/	car, week
/ow/	phone, no		/l/	late, call
/ɔ/	call,* short		/m/	make, lamp
/ɔy/	join, boy		/n/	near, sun
/ʊ/	book, put		/ŋ/	long, working
/uw/	soon, too		/p/	pay, keep
/ə/	up, cut, ago		/r/	rain, there
/ər/	word, first, answer		/s/	same, nice
			/ʃ/	should, push
			/t/	talk, light
			/tʃ/	chair, watch
			/v/	very, live
			/w/	walk, swim
			/y/	yes, you
			/z/	zoo, easy
			/ʒ/	television, usual
			/θ/	thanks, bath

*Many Americans and Canadians say this word with the vowel /ɑ/.

Authors' acknowledgments

We would like to thank:

Jane Mairs, Sue André, and Janet Battiste for their meticulous editing and for their professionalism and patience in guiding the manuscript to its present form.

Jeanne McCarten, Lindsay White, and Alison Silver, who similarly guided the British edition of this book and whose influence still remains in these pages, and Mary Vaughn, who initiated this North American edition.

The many people who commented on the material and the principles on which it is based, in particular Michael McCarthy, David Brazil, and Richard Cauldwell.

Jim Rader, Marjorie Fuchs, and the anonymous reviewer, for their valuable comments and suggestions.

To the student

Who is this book for?

Pronunciation Plus is for intermediate-level students of North American English who want to improve their pronunciation. Many of the activities would also be useful for higher-level students.

The book has been written for students working in a class with a teacher, although many of the tasks can be used by students working on their own with a cassette recorder.

What is the approach of this book?

Pronunciation Plus uses many different types of activities to teach pronunciation. The activities are intended to help you become more aware of your own pronunciation and the pronunciation of native speakers of North American English. You will be asked to identify, predict, and use various features of English pronunciation and to discover rules, solve puzzles, and exchange information with other students.

How is the book organized?

The book is divided into an introduction and eight parts. The introduction shows how to ask about and check pronunciation. Each of the eight parts of the book focuses on a particular aspect of English pronunciation: vowel sounds, consonant sounds, consonant clusters, word stress and rhythm, changes that take place in conversational speech, intonation, the pronunciation of common grammatical elements, and the connection between spelling and pronunciation. Each part is divided into six to eight units.

It is not necessary to work from Unit 1 to Unit 60. You or your teacher can choose the units or parts that will help with the pronunciation problems you have. Keep in mind that difficulties with pronunciation often involve two or more features – for example, vowel sounds and word stress – and the way these features work together.

When do you listen to the tape?

Many of the tasks in this book involve listening to material on tape. Listening to the tape will give you the opportunity to hear and imitate a variety of native speakers, pronouncing words in isolation as well as in connected speech. When you see this symbol ▣, it is time to listen to the tape.

In addition to listening to and repeating after the recording, you can try reading the material in your book aloud at the same time that the tape is playing. This can be helpful, especially in improving fluency. First read over the material in your book until you are familiar with it. Then read aloud along with the tape, trying to use the same speed and rhythm as the speakers on the recording.

Introduction
Asking about pronunciation

Here are some ways of asking how to pronounce words correctly.

Asking about the pronunciation of written words

 1 Listen to these conversations.

2 Work in pairs. Ask about the pronunciation of these words.

> temperature   commercial   chocolate
> accidentally   vegetables   psychologist

3 Listen and check your pronunciation of the words.

Asking if your pronunciation is correct

4 Listen to these conversations.

5 Work in pairs. Use the phrases in the conversations to ask about the pronunciation of these cities in the United States.

Chicago   Los Angeles   Miami   Seattle
Phoenix   Minneapolis   Hartford

 6 Listen and check your pronunciation of the names.

Asking which pronunciation is correct

 7 Listen to these conversations.

8 Are there words that you are not sure how to pronounce? Ask your teacher about them in the same way.

Asking about pronunciation / Introduction

Unit 1

The vowels /æ/ (hat), /ɪ/ (big), and /ɛ/ (red)

1 Repeat these words. Notice the sound /æ/ in each.

> back   map   plan   class   match

2 Underline the vowels pronounced /æ/ in this conversation.

A: Where were you standing?
B: At the gas station.
A: Where was the man?
B: He ran out of the bank.
A: Did he have anything in his hand?
B: A black bag.
A: Thank you, ma'am.

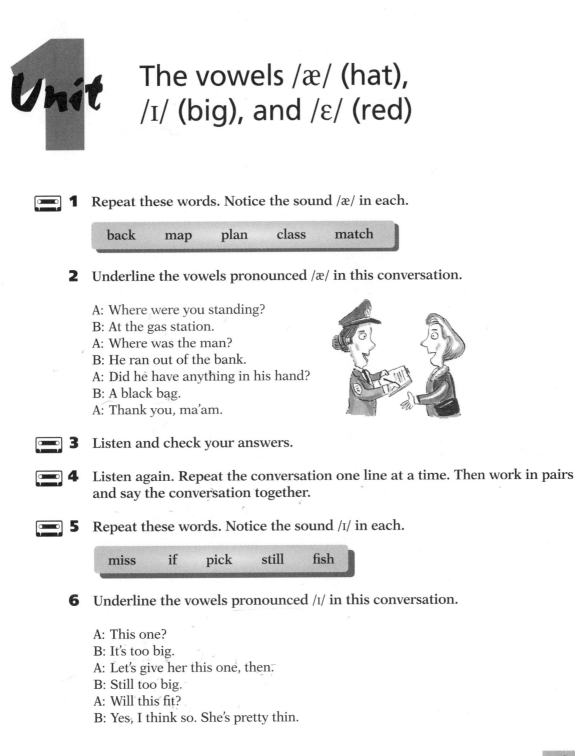

3 Listen and check your answers.

4 Listen again. Repeat the conversation one line at a time. Then work in pairs and say the conversation together.

5 Repeat these words. Notice the sound /ɪ/ in each.

> miss   if   pick   still   fish

6 Underline the vowels pronounced /ɪ/ in this conversation.

A: This one?
B: It's too big.
A: Let's give her this one, then.
B: Still too big.
A: Will this fit?
B: Yes, I think so. She's pretty thin.

7 Listen and check your answers.

8 Listen again. Repeat the conversation one line at a time. Then work in pairs and say the conversation together.

9 Repeat these words. Notice the sound /ɛ/ in each.

> yes   red   tell   best   help

10 Underline the vowels pronounced /ɛ/ in this conversation.

A: And can you get some red peppers?
B: How many?
A: Ten or twelve.
B: Anything else?
A: Some bread. Do you need any money?
B: No, I'll pay by check.

11 Listen and check your answers.

12 Listen again. Repeat the conversation one line at a time. Then work in pairs and say the conversation together.

13 Write the words in the box in the spaces next to the pictures.

> a map   a television   a sweater   a credit card   stamps
> a tennis racket   a camera   a blanket   a fishing rod
> some cash   a flashlight   a tent   matches   a hat
> your address book   scissors   a backpack   some string
> something to drink   an interesting magazine

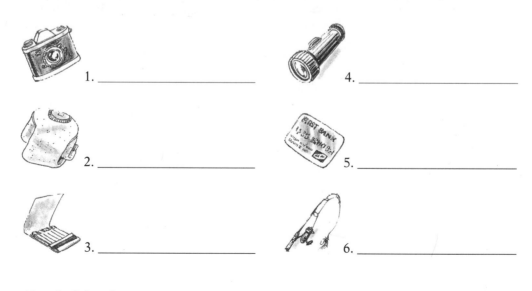

1. _____

4. _____

2. _____

5. _____

3. _____

6. _____

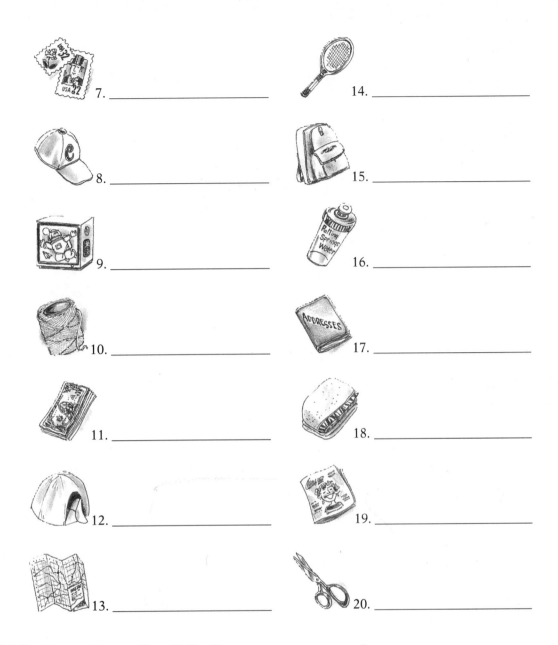

7. _____

8. _____

9. _____

10. _____

11. _____

12. _____

13. _____

14. _____

15. _____

16. _____

17. _____

18. _____

19. _____

20. _____

14 Repeat the words and check your answers.

15 Work in pairs. Discuss with your partner the three most important things to have when . . .

1. you are lost in a city
2. you are on vacation
3. your car breaks down
4. you are lost in the woods

Choose words from the box in **13**.

16 Report your answers to the rest of the class.

Unit 2

The vowels /ɑ/ (father), /ə/ (bus), and /ʊ/ (book)

1 Repeat these words.

just	push
stop	lunch
pull	block

watch*	good
looks	stuck
shut	stopped

blood	book
car	start
cook	cut

* Some Americans and Canadians use the vowel /ɔ/ in this word.

2 Match the words in each box that have the same vowel sound.

3 Repeat the words and check your answers.

4 Complete these conversations using the pairs of matching words in **1**.

1. A: Is Molly here?
   B: No. She ___*just*___ went out to ___*lunch*___.

2. A: Do you like it?
   B: Yes, it _____ _____.

3. A: Does the bus _____ here?
   B: No, on the next _____.

4. A: Can't you _____ the door?
   B: No, it's _____.

5. A: Is that _____?

   B: Yeah, I _____ my finger.

6. A: What time is it?

   B: Sorry, my _____ has _____.

7. A: What are you reading?

   B: It's a _____ _____.

8. A: I can't open the door.

   B: _____ it. Don't _____ it!

9. A: What's the matter?

   B: The _____ won't _____.

5 Listen and check your answers.

6 Listen again. Repeat the conversations one line at a time. Then work in pairs and say the conversations together.

7 Repeat the words on the left.

1. common	*a common problem* ,	_____
2. good	*a good book* ,	_____
3. comfortable	_____ ,	_____
4. hard	_____ ,	_____
5. funny	_____ ,	_____

Work in pairs. Think of two things that these adjectives can describe. Write the answers in the spaces.

8 Report your answers to the rest of the class.

Unit B

/ɪ/ and /ɛ/; /æ/ and /ə/

Focus on /ɪ/ and /ɛ/

 1 Repeat these words.

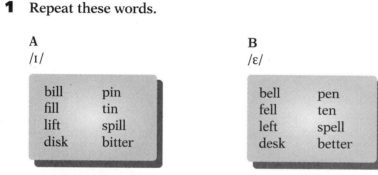

A
/ɪ/

bill	pin
fill	tin
lift	spill
disk	bitter

B
/ɛ/

bell	pen
fell	ten
left	spell
desk	better

2 Work in pairs. Say a word from one of the boxes. Your partner will tell you if it comes from box A or box B.

3 Listen to these sentences. Do they contain words from box A or box B? Write the word you hear in the space.

1. They ___fell___ in the hole.
2. Can I have the _____, please?
3. I _____ the books at the library.
4. It was too expensive to buy _____.
5. Put the file on this _____.
6. Is this tea _____?
7. I found a _____ on the floor.
8. You don't _____ *orange juice* like that.

Focus on /æ/ and /ə/

4 The words in these phrases contain the sounds /æ/ and /ə/ in four different patterns. (Ignore the words *a* and *an*.) Listen.

An angry customer. = /æ/ + /ə/
Run faster! = /ə/ + /æ/
Enough money. = /ə/ + /ə/
A happy man. = /æ/ + /æ/

Now listen to more phrases with /æ/ and /ə/ and write each one in the correct column in the table.

/æ/ + /ə/	/ə/ + /æ/	/ə/ + /ə/	/æ/ + /æ/
		someplace sunny	a black jacket

5 Listen again. Repeat the phrases and check your answers.

6 Use some of the phrases from **4** to complete these conversations.

What did you do on the weekend?

Where do you work?

What was he wearing?

Where did you go last night?

What made you late?

When did you get married?

Who's at the door?

7 Work in pairs and say the conversations together.

The vowels /iy/ (see), /ey/ (train), /ɔ/ (call), /ow/ (no), and /uw/ (two)

1 Repeat these words. Notice the sound of the underlined vowels.

/iy/	/ey/	/ɔ/	/ow/	/uw/
tree	day	saw*	know	blue
jeans	rain	morning	phone	June
beach	late	walk*	coat	suit
leave	gave	door	drove	pool

*Many Americans and Canadians use the vowel /ɑ/ in these words.

2 Work in pairs to complete the table. How many of these vowel sounds are there in the words in each row? Write the number of times each vowel occurs.

	/iy/	/ey/	/ɔ/*	/ow/	/uw/
1. slow, choose, law, boat, famous		1	1	2	1
2. clean, complain, piece, great, fruit					
3. coast, water, waiter, lost, most					
4. neighbor, daughter, receive, thought, group					
5. food, improve, home, feel, fall					
6. date, speak, delay, break, change					

*Many Americans and Canadians pronounce the words in this column with the vowel /ɑ/.

3 Repeat the words and check your answers.

4 Cover up the story on page 11. Look at the pictures and listen to the story. Say "Stop!" when you hear a mistake, and say what is wrong.

One morning last April, Susan was still sleeping when the doorbell rang. It was her friend Dave inviting her to go to the beach for a picnic. Later that morning, Susan left her house and walked to the station to catch the bus. She was wearing a T-shirt and shorts, since it was quite warm. As she sat on the bus, she looked out the door. She saw some sheep in a field. It was starting to snow.

Before long, the snow stopped and the sun came out. Susan arrived at the pool and met Steve. They walked down to the beach and had their picnic next to a tree. They had coffee and cake, and Steve painted a picture. They had a really nice evening.

5 Work in pairs. Read the story and discuss the mistakes. Correct them like this:

April is wrong. It should be *June*.
Doorbell is wrong. It should be *phone*.

6 Cover up the story and retell it using the pictures.

Unit 5

/æ/ and /ɑ/; /ɪ/ and /iy/

Focus on /æ/ and /ɑ/

1 Repeat these words. Notice the sound of the underlined vowels.

/æ/

cat
camping
stamps
hats
Spanish

/ɑ/

jogs
hobby
hospital
farm
guitar

2 Find someone in your class who . . .

1. has a cat _____
2. jogs _____
3. speaks Spanish _____
4. likes to go camping _____
5. can play the guitar _____
6. collects stamps _____
7. grew up on a farm _____
8. wears hats _____
9. has an unusual hobby _____
10. has never stayed in a hospital _____

Ask questions like these:

Do you have a cat?
Do you like to go camping?
Did you grow up on a farm?

Write the name of the person who fits the description in the space.

3 Report your answers to the rest of the class. For example:

Nadia has a cat.

Focus on /ɪ/ and /iy/

4 Repeat these words. Notice the sound of the underlined vowels.

India	river	cheese	Chinese	green
fourteen	knee	musician	British	teacher
milk	pink	chicken	swimming	finger
Egypt	skiing	tea	stream	a million

5 Listen to the words again. If the underlined vowel is pronounced /ɪ/ (as in *big*), circle the vowel. If the vowel is pronounced /iy/ (as in *see*), do nothing.

Complete these sentences:

Spellings for the sound /iy/ usually include the letter _____. (Exception: *ski*)

The sound /ɪ/ is usually spelled with the letter _____.

6 Work in pairs. From the words in the box, find two . . .

1. things to eat
2. jobs
3. countries
4. numbers
5. colors
6. sports
7. parts of the body
8. nationalities
9. things containing water
10. things to drink

7 Compare answers with the rest of the class. For example:

Two things to eat are cheese and chicken.

Unit 6

/ə/, /ʊ/, and /uw/; /ɑ/ and /ɔ/

Focus on /ə/, /ʊ/, and /uw/

1 All the words in the box include the letter *u*. How is it pronounced? Write the words in the table.

include	/ə/ cup	/ʊ/ good	/uw/ two
customer			
full			
supermarket			
June			
uncle			
pull			
Sunday			
flu			
put			
push			
number			

2 Repeat the words and check your answers.

3 Work in pairs. Draw arrows to connect the sentences. Make five 2-line conversations.

1. Where should I put your luggage?
2. But I bought a new tube on Tuesday.
3. You'll be too hot in the sun.
4. My brother. Would you like me to introduce you?
5. Thanks. It's from a really good cookbook.
6. There isn't much toothpaste left.
7. In the trunk. I just have one suitcase.
8. I think I'll put on my wool suit.
9. Who's that in the blue uniform?
10. That onion soup was wonderful.

4 Repeat the conversations one line at a time and check your answers. Then work in pairs and say the conversations together.

5 Underline all the /ə/, /ʊ/, and /uw/ sounds in the sentences. How many of each can you find? Add the words to the table in **1**.

Focus on /ɑ/ and /ɔ/

6 Some words are pronounced differently in different parts of North America. For example, the words in the box are pronounced with the vowel /ɔ/ (as in *short*, *dog*, or *call*) by most people from New York, but they are pronounced with /ɑ/ (as in *father* or *hot*) by most people from California.

California   New York

Listen to these words, first pronounced by someone from New York and then by someone from California.

saw	bought	caught	lost	called	dog	walk	long
office	talked	mall	coffee	daughter	cough	awful
wrong	Boston	lawn	softball	exhausted

7 Listen to these people talking about their weekend. Focus on the underlined vowels. Where do you think each speaker comes from – New York or California? Put a check in the correct column.

	New York	California
1. I took my dog for a long walk in the park.	☑	❑
2. I saw an awful movie.	❑	❑
3. I went to the mall and bought a picture for my office.	❑	❑
4. Oh, I went to the mall, too. I bought a new coffeepot.	❑	❑
5. I caught a cold with a bad cough, so I just stayed home.	❑	❑
6. I taught my daughter how to ride a bike.	❑	❑
7. I took the wrong bus and got lost yesterday.	❑	❑
8. I called my friend in Boston. We talked for almost an hour.	❑	❑
9. Yesterday I played softball, then I did laundry, and then I mowed the lawn. I'm still exhausted.	❑	❑

8 Work in pairs. Talk about a busy weekend that you had. Use some of the words in the box in **6**. Use the vowel that your teacher uses in these words. Which vowel does your teacher use? Where is your teacher from?

Unit 7 /ey/ and /ɛ/; /ow/ and /ɔ/

Focus on /ey/ and /ɛ/

1 Look at the words in the box. Underline the vowels pronounced /ey/ (as in
day and _rain_), and circle the vowels pronounced /ɛ/ (as in _red_).

potato	dentist	Mexico	November	seven
eight	painter	radio	train	Asia	May
sweater	Spain	yellow	table	gray	head
helicopter	South America	bed	embassy
bread	television	dress	brain	station

2 Repeat the words and check your answers.

3 Work with a partner. Potato and bread are both things to eat. Find more
pairs using the words in the box in **1**.

4 Compare answers with the rest of the class.

Focus on /ow/ and /ɔ/

5 Repeat these words. Notice the sound of the underlined vowels.

/ow/

clothes	snowing	smoke
old	hole	closed
phone	cold	wardrobe

/ɔ/

corner	fall*	drawing*
walking*	daughter*	bald*
floor	warmly	wardrobe

*Many Americans and Canadians pronounce these words with the vowel /ɑ/.

6 Use as many of the words in **5** as you can to describe the pictures.

7 What other words that contain the sounds /ow/ or /ɔ/ can you use to describe the pictures?

/ər/ (word); vowels followed by r (car, short, chair, near)

1 When /r/ comes after /ə/, it changes the way /ə/ sounds.

🔊 Repeat these words. They all have the sound /ər/.

learn	first	worst	nervous	work	return	earn
dirty	girl	early	curly	sir	vertical	

2 Work in pairs. Fill in the crossword puzzle with words from the box in **1**. The answers are words that are *opposites* of the clues.

Across
- 3 calm
- 5 clean
- 7 teach
- 9 ma'am or miss
- 10 best
- 11 straight
- 12 boy

Down
- 1 leave
- 2 last
- 4 horizontal
- 6 late
- 8 spend
- 10 relax

3 Compare answers with the rest of the class.

🔊 **4** Repeat these words. Do not touch the roof of your mouth for /r/.

/ər/	/ɑr/	/ɔr/	/ɛr/	/ɪr/
word	hard	bored	hair	here
bird	farm	form	air	ear
heard	heart	court	care	year
burn	barn	warm	wear	clearly

5 Listen to these words. Do you hear the word in column A or the one in column B? Put a check in the correct box.

	A	B		A	B		A	B
1.	hurt ☐	heart ☐	5.	bird ☐	bored ☐	9.	heart ☐	hot ☐
2.	shirts ☐	shorts ☐	6.	burn ☐	barn ☐	10.	farm ☐	form ☐
3.	bird ☐	bud ☐	7.	shirt ☐	shut ☐	11.	ear ☐	air ☐
4.	work ☐	walk ☐	8.	her ☐	hair ☐	12.	court ☐	caught ☐

6 In each line, four of the words have the same vowel sound, and one has a different vowel sound. This is the *odd one out*. Work in pairs and try to find the odd one out in each line.

1. work, Thursday, early, clearly, prefer
2. park, heard, hard, farm, heart
3. here, near, wear, year, hear
4. chair, large, care, pair, their
5. story, warm, word, four, door

7 Repeat the words and check your answers.

8 Here are some photographs of Ernie. The two pictures on top show Ernie fourteen years ago, at home and at work. The two pictures on the bottom show Ernie now. What things have changed?

/p/ (pay), /b/ (back), /t/ (talk), /d/ (dance), /k/ (car), and /g/ (give)

1 To make the sounds underlined in these words, part of the mouth is completely closed and then the air behind it is suddenly released.

Repeat these words.

/p/	/b/	/t/	/d/	/k/	/g/
pay	back	talk	dance	keep	guess
paper	business	tennis	different	color	going
repeat	baby	return	address	occur	again

2 When these sounds occur at the end of a word, the air is often *not* released.

Repeat these words.

pipe	job	tight	dead	cook	dog

3 The pictures show how these six consonants are made. Look at the position of the tongue and lips in each picture. Which sounds are shown in **a**, **b**, and **c**? Each picture shows *two* sounds.

a. b. c.

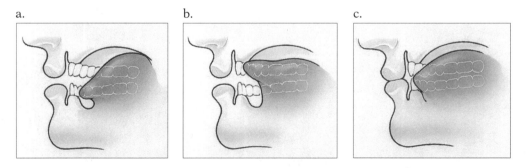

Now place your hand on your throat as you say the two sounds shown in each picture. How are the two sounds different?

4 Todd, Debbie, Kate, Gabe, Pat, and Barbara are thinking about the presents they would like for their birthdays. Todd wants things that begin with the sound /t/, Debbie with the sound /d/, Kate with the sound /k/, and so on. What presents do they each want? Make sentences like these:

> Todd wants a tennis racket.
> Barbara wants some boots.

Who wants the most presents? Who wants the fewest presents? Can you suggest some other presents they might like?

5 The difference between the consonants /p/ and /b/, /t/ and /d/, and /k/ and /g/ *at the end of a word* can be hard to hear. The main difference is in the length of the vowel sound before the consonant. Vowels are *shorter* before final consonants pronounced without the voice (like /t/), and *longer* before final consonants pronounced using the voice (like /d/).

Repeat these words.

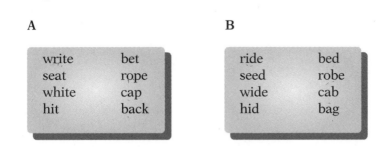

A

write	bet
seat	rope
white	cap
hit	back

B

ride	bed
seed	robe
wide	cab
hid	bag

6 Listen to these words. Do you hear a word from box A or box B? Write *A* or *B* in the space.

1. _____   3. _____   5. _____   7. _____
2. _____   4. _____   6. _____   8. _____

7 Work in pairs. Say a word from one of the boxes. Your partner will tell you if it comes from box A or box B.

8 Listen to these sentences. Do they contain words from box A or box B (in **5**)? Write the word you hear in the space.

1. We bought a _____ table.
2. She's learning to _____.
3. Where can I get a _____ around here?
4. The _____ is behind the door.
5. I put it in the _____.
6. Who made the _____?
7. We need one more _____.
8. The boy _____ the ball.

9 Repeat these words.

A

deep	dangerous	good
beautiful	boring	bad
colorful	comfortable	
quiet	patient	terrible
big	dark	

B

dentist	doctor	garden
bed	cave	camera
cook	party	pain
tiger	television	town
teacher	dinner	

10 Work in pairs. Add words from box A to words from box B to find . . .

1. something that is frightening (for example, a deep cave)
2. something that is expensive
3. someone who does a good job
4. someone who does not do a good job
5. something you like
6. something you don't like

11 Report your answers to the rest of the class.

/t/ and /d/; /p/ and /b/

Focus on /t/ and /d/

 1 Listen to these words. They all contain both the sound /t/ and the sound /d/. If the sound /t/ comes first, write *t*. If the sound /d/ comes first, write *d*. For example, if you heard the word *admit* you would write *d*; if you heard the word *outside* you would write *t*.

1. _____	4. _____	7. _____
2. _____	5. _____	8. _____
3. _____	6. _____	9. _____

2 Sometimes the letters *t* and *d* are pronounced the same in North American English – like a very quick /d/ (called a *flap* or a *tap*). This happens when *t* or *d* comes after a vowel or /r/ sound and before an unstressed vowel.

The words in each of these pairs usually sound the same. Listen.

latter = ladder
liter = leader
putting = pudding

3 Repeat these words. The letters pronounced as a flap are underlined.

> shortest   tightest   wettest   driest   saddest

4 Underline the letters *t* and *d* in these words that are pronounced as a flap.

> hottest   coldest   smartest   oldest   dullest   hardest
> tallest   most exciting   most beautiful   city

5 Listen and check your answers.

6 Listen again. Repeat the words.

7 Work in pairs. Ask and answer these questions. Take notes on your partner's answers.

1. What's the coldest place you've ever been?
2. What's the hottest place you've ever been?
3. What's the most exciting city you've ever been to?
4. What's the most beautiful place you've ever been to?
5. What's the hardest course you've ever taken?
6. What's the dullest course you've ever taken?
7. Who's the oldest person you know?
8. Who's the tallest person you know?
9. Who's the smartest person you know?

8 Report your partner's answers to the rest of the class. For example:

The coldest place Mario's ever been is . . .

Focus on /p/ *and* /b/

9 Work in pairs. Match the words on the left with the words on the right to describe what you see in the picture.

a pile of   pie
a book of   perfume
a basket of   pajamas
a piece of   stamps
a box of   pencils
a bar of   soup
a bag of   pears
a pair of   potato chips
a bottle of   bricks
a bunch of   pasta
a plate of   soap
a bowl of   grapes

10 Repeat and check your answers.

11 Can you think of any other ways of completing the phrases on the left in **9**? The words you add should contain either the sound /p/ or the sound /b/.

/s/ (same), /z/ (zoo), /f/ (four), /v/ (very), /θ/ (thanks), and /ð/ (this)

1 To make the sounds underlined in these words, air is pushed through a narrow opening in the mouth. Repeat these words.

/s/	/z/	/f/	/v/	/θ/	/ð/
same	zoo	few	voice	thanks	this
second	zero	phone	very	thought	that
sister	easy	perfect	never	Thursday	those
house	noise	enough	five	nothing	breathe
science	amuse	February	invite	fourth	other

2 The pictures show how the sounds are made. Which two sounds are shown in **a**, **b**, and **c**?

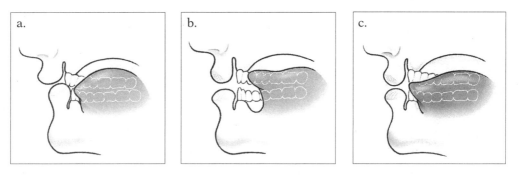

a.   b.   c.

3 Listen to these words. Do you hear the word in column A or the one in column B? Put a check in the correct box.

	A		B			A		B	
1.	fat	❏	that	❏	8.	closing	❏	clothing	❏
2.	sing	❏	thing	❏	9.	there	❏	fair	❏
3.	say	❏	they	❏	10.	Sue	❏	zoo	❏
4.	some	❏	thumb	❏	11.	few	❏	view	❏
5.	first	❏	thirst	❏	12.	prices	❏	prizes	❏
6.	breeze	❏	breathe	❏	13.	ice	❏	eyes	❏
7.	pass	❏	path	❏	14.	leaf	❏	leave	❏

4 Work with a partner. Look at each pair of words in **3**. Your partner should say one of the words *silently* to you. Tell your partner which word you think was said. For items 10 to 14, your partner should say one of the words in each pair *aloud*. Can you explain why you need to say these words aloud?

5   Work in pairs. Discuss with your partner how to say these numbers.

1st	77	2nd	3rd	443	
5th	4,000	2/16/57	12/15/2006	
14th	XXXV	XLVI	MMM	

6   Repeat and check your answers.

7   Work in pairs. First say the dates on the right. For example, for the first one say:

July fourth

Then match the U.S. holidays or events on the left with the dates on the right.

1. New Year's Day   7/4
2. Valentine's Day   3/20
3. the first day of spring   10/12
4. the first day of fall   10/31
5. Independence Day   1/1
6. Christmas   9/22
7. Halloween   11/11
8. Columbus Day   2/14
9. St. Patrick's Day   12/25
10. Veterans Day   3/17

8   Compare answers with the rest of the class. For example:

New Year's Day is January first.

Unit 12

/θ/ and /ð/; /f/, /v/, /p/, and /b/

Focus on /θ/ *and* /ð/

1 Repeat these sentences.

1. Three thirty.
2. It's through there.
3. Are they brothers?
4. The twenty-third.

5. When does it get there?
6. Is that Tom and Matthew over there?
7. When is Thanksgiving?
8. Thanks.

2 Work in pairs. Write the sentences in **1** in the spaces in these conversations. Then say the conversations together.

1. A: Where's the bathroom?
   B: _____
   A: _____
   B: You're welcome.

2. A: _____
   B: It's the fourth Thursday in November.
   A: What date is that this year?
   B: _____

3. A: What time's the train to Fort Worth?
   B: _____
   A: _____
   B: Four twenty-three.

4. A: _____
   B: Yes, they're always together.
   A: _____
   B: I think so.

Focus on /f/, /v/, /p/, and /b/

3 Listen to these words. Do you hear the word in column A or the one in column B? Put a check in the correct box.

	A		B			A		B	
1.	boat	❑	vote	❑	6.	pool	❑	fool	❑
2.	past	❑	fast	❑	7.	cup	❑	cuff	❑
3.	blood	❑	flood	❑	8.	best	❑	vest	❑
4.	bet	❑	vet	❑	9.	cheap	❑	chief	❑
5.	bill	❑	fill	❑	10.	curb	❑	curve	❑

4 Work in pairs. Your partner should say one of the words in each pair *silently* to you. Try to decide which one is being said. Take turns being listener and speaker.

5 Repeat these words.

> the telephone   the bicycle   the elevator   television   photography
> the microscope   the automobile   the printing press   vaccination
> frozen food   movies   the ballpoint pen   the VCR   the airplane
> the personal computer   vitamins   the microwave oven   the zipper

6 The pictures below show *some* of the things in **5**. Which are they? Write the words in the spaces.

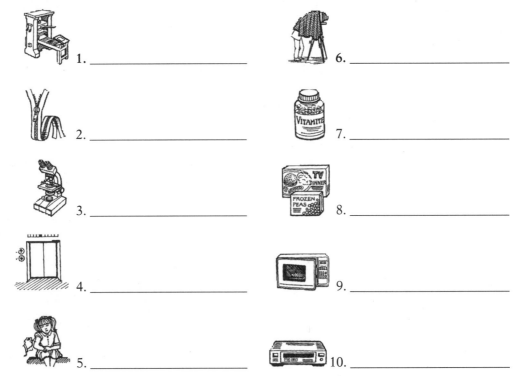

1. _____

2. _____

3. _____

4. _____

5. _____

6. _____

7. _____

8. _____

9. _____

10. _____

7 Work in pairs. When do you think the items in **5** were invented or discovered? Write the name of the item in the space next to the year.

Here are some phrases to help you:

> I think . . . was invented in . . . .
> When was . . . discovered?

Inventions and Discoveries

1450 _____

1590 _____

1796 _____

1841 _____

1857 _____

1876 _____

1884 _____

1891 _____ and _____

1893 _____

1903 _____

1912 _____

1924 _____

1926 _____

1944 _____

1947 _____

1975 _____ and _____

8 Compare answers with the rest of the class.

Unit 13

/ʃ/ (should), /tʃ/ (chair), /ʒ/ (television), and /dʒ/ (job)

1 To make the sounds underlined in these words, the tongue is touching (/tʃ/ and /dʒ/) or almost touching (/ʃ/ and /ʒ/) the roof of the mouth. Repeat these words.

/ʃ/	/tʃ/	/ʒ/	/dʒ/
shopping	check	television	June
vacation	kitchen	pleasure	jewelry
dishes	furniture	garage	agency
cash	beach	usually	college

2 Work in pairs to ask and answer questions like this:

A: Where would you usually catch a train?
B: At a train station.

Where would you usually . . .

1. catch a train?   At a furniture store.
2. arrange a vacation?   At a bank.
3. buy a couch?   At a college.
4. wash dishes?   In the garage.
5. keep cheese?   At a jewelry store.
6. study a foreign language?   In the kitchen.
7. cash a check?   At the beach.
8. find seashells?   At a travel agency.
9. buy a gold chain?   At a train station.
10. keep a car?   In the refrigerator.

3 Repeat these words.

peaches	sugar	orange juice	jam	chicken	cherries
spinach	french fries	champagne	fish	mushrooms	
cabbage	cheeseburger	fresh vegetables	milkshake		
cheese	chocolate	sausage	chips		

4 Listen to this doctor talking to her patient. The patient has said that he feels tired all the time, and the doctor is now asking him about his diet. In the box in **3**, put a check next to the foods and drinks that you hear them talking about.

5 Work in pairs. Write a diet sheet for the patient in the conversation. List things he should eat or drink and things he should not eat or drink. Include words from the box in **3**.

Unit 14 /w/ (walk), /y/ (yes), /l/ (late), and /r/ (rain)

 1 Repeat these words.

/w/	/y/	/l/	/r/
walk	you	late	rain
windy	year	alone	right
would	yesterday	call	remember
when	museum	clock	restaurant
twenty	view	little	friend

2 Underline all the /w/ sounds in this conversation. Can you find any *w* letters that are not pronounced /w/?

A: What's the weather like?
B: Awful. It's wet and windy.
A: Should we go for a walk anyway?
B: Let's wait twenty minutes.

3 Listen and check your answers.

4 Listen again. Repeat the conversation one line at a time. Then work in pairs and say the conversation together.

5 Underline all the /y/ sounds in this conversation. Can you find any /y/ sounds that are not written with the letter *y*?

A: I had an interview yesterday.
B: At the university?
A: Yes, in the music department.
B: Do you know if you got the job?
A: No, I don't know yet.

6 Listen and check your answers.

7 Listen again. Repeat the conversation one line at a time. Then work in pairs and say the conversation together.

8 Underline all the /l/ sounds in this conversation. Can you find any *l* letters that are not pronounced /l/?

A: Would you like to have lunch?
B: It's a little early.
A: It's almost twelve o'clock.
B: Let's wait till twelve thirty.
A: Well, OK. But no later, or I'll be late for class.

9 Listen and check your answers.

10 Listen again. Repeat the conversation one line at a time. Then work in pairs and say the conversation together.

11 Underline all the /r/ sounds in this conversation.

A: Did you remember to call Ray?
B: I tried three times on Friday.
A: He was probably at the library.
B: You're probably right. I'll try again tomorrow.

12 Listen and check your answers.

13 Listen again. Repeat the conversation one line at a time. Then work in pairs and say the conversation together.

14 Listen to this conversation while you look at the table on the next page. Will is asking Laura about her vacation. When you hear the answers to the questions on the left, write the answers in column A. Use words from the boxes on the right.

	A	B	
Where?	*Florida*		Florida, New York, Washington, Italy, France
With whom?			with family, alone, with a friend, with a tour group
Hotel?	*small*		clean, comfortable, swimming pool, large, small, old, quiet, luxurious, uncomfortable, dirty, terrible
Things to do?			swimming, walking, windsurfing, relaxing, driving, restaurants, museums
Weather?			cool, warm, cloudy, rainy, wet, windy, really hot, cold, beautiful, wonderful, terrible, lousy

15 Choose words and phrases from the boxes on the right to describe an imaginary vacation. Write these words and phrases in column B. Then work in pairs and talk about your vacation with your partner. For example:

Where did you go for vacation? I went to Italy.
Who did you go with? I went with my family.
What did you do there? I went to a lot of museums and restaurants.

/w/ and /v/; /l/ and /r/

Focus on /w/ and /v/

1 Cover the sentences on the left. Listen to the five sentences. How many /v/ sounds do you hear in each? Write your answer in the space.

    1. I only have twelve. _____

    2. She works hard every day. _____

    3. We had to drive up on the sidewalk to avoid him. _____

    4. I lost my wallet, traveler's checks, and visa. _____

    5. We're having visitors over the weekend. _____

2 Uncover the sentences and check your answers.

3 Listen again. Repeat the sentences.

4 Cover these sentences and listen. How many /w/ sounds do you hear in each sentence? Write your answer in the space.

    1. What's this one over here? _____

    2. Was everything made of wood? _____

    3. It's quite warm for November. _____

    4. They're having a quiet wedding next Wednesday. _____

    5. It was very wet last week, wasn't it? _____

5 Uncover the sentences and check your answers.

6 Listen again. Repeat the sentences.

Focus on /l/ and /r/

7 The pictures on page 35 show how the sounds /l/ and /r/ are made. Which sound is shown in **a**? Which sound is shown in **b**?

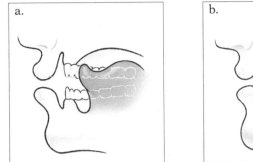
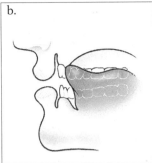

 8 Repeat these words.

/l/

light   left turn   lane
allowed   unload   only
school   hill   children
slippery   carefully
parking lot

/r/

road   right turn   rains
narrower   crossing
straight   street   traffic circle
trucks   pedestrians
railroad   cars

9 Work in pairs to decide what these road signs mean. Put a check in the correct box.

1.

❑ No left turns are allowed.
☑ No right turns are allowed.
❑ Don't turn right if the light is red.

2.

❑ The road curves to the left.
❑ All cars should keep to the right.
❑ The road is slippery when it rains.

3.

❑ Do not go around other cars.
❑ The road will get narrower on the right.
❑ There is a bridge ahead.

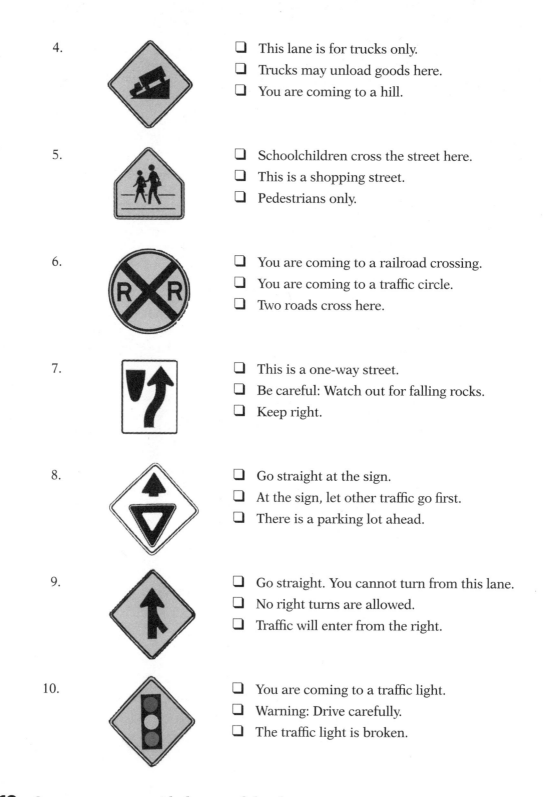

4. ❑ This lane is for trucks only.
   ❑ Trucks may unload goods here.
   ❑ You are coming to a hill.

5. ❑ Schoolchildren cross the street here.
   ❑ This is a shopping street.
   ❑ Pedestrians only.

6. ❑ You are coming to a railroad crossing.
   ❑ You are coming to a traffic circle.
   ❑ Two roads cross here.

7. ❑ This is a one-way street.
   ❑ Be careful: Watch out for falling rocks.
   ❑ Keep right.

8. ❑ Go straight at the sign.
   ❑ At the sign, let other traffic go first.
   ❑ There is a parking lot ahead.

9. ❑ Go straight. You cannot turn from this lane.
   ❑ No right turns are allowed.
   ❑ Traffic will enter from the right.

10. ❑ You are coming to a traffic light.
    ❑ Warning: Drive carefully.
    ❑ The traffic light is broken.

10 Compare answers with the rest of the class.

/m/ (make), /n/ (near), and /ŋ/ (long)

1 To make the sounds underlined in these words, part of the mouth is completely closed by the lips or tongue, and air is allowed to pass through the nose.

Repeat these words.

/m/	/n/	/ŋ/
music	never	long
home	mine	nothing
climb	once	think
museum	doesn't	finger
sometimes	mountain	singing

2 Write the sentences from the box next to the pictures to describe what **Sam** is doing in each.

He's ironing.	He's cooking.	He's listening to music.
He's washing dishes.	He's jogging	He's cleaning the bathroom.
He's painting.	He's gardening.	He's vacuuming the living room.
He's shopping.	He's doing laundry.	

1. _____

2. _____

3. _____

4. _____

5. _____

6. _____

7. _____

8. _____

9. _____

10. _____

11. _____

3 Repeat the sentences and check your answers.

4 How good is your memory? Work in pairs. Study the pictures in **2** for one minute and then close your book. Try to remember what Sam likes doing and what he doesn't like doing. Report to your partner like this:

> He likes cooking.
> He doesn't like washing dishes.

Your partner will check your answers.

5 Write the names of three classmates in the spaces at the top of the columns. Interview them to find out what they do on weekends.

Ask questions like these:

Do you ever go jogging?	No, never.
	Yes, sometimes.
How often do you watch television?	Every weekend.
	I never watch television.

Write *E* if the person answers "every weekend," *O* if the person answers "often," *S* for "sometimes," or *N̄* for "never."

	Name _____	Name _____	Name _____
go jogging			
watch television			
go dancing			
listen to music			
go shopping			
clean your house			
work in the garden			
go to museums			
go swimming			
go mountain climbing			
stay home and do nothing			

6 Report your answers to the rest of the class. For example:

> Kumiko goes jogging every weekend.
> Juan sometimes goes to museums.

Discuss which activities were the most popular. Were there differences between what men did and what women did on weekends? Were there activities that none of the people you interviewed did?

A CONSONANT CLUSTER *occurs when two or more* CONSONANT SOUNDS *come together. For example, the word* spell *begins with the consonant cluster* /sp/, *and the word* thinks *ends with the consonant cluster* /ŋks/.

Consonant letters and consonant sounds

1 Underline the parts of the words where there are two or more CONSONANT LETTERS together. Then complete the first column with the number of consonant letters you have underlined.

	Number of consonant letters	Number of consonant sounds		Number of consonant letters	Number of consonant sounds
1. blood	2	2	7. right		
2. against	3	3	8. next		
3. ticket	2	1	9. there		
4. school			10. walk		
5. dollar			11. film		
6. chair			12. street		

2 Now listen to the words. Complete the second column with the number of consonant sounds you hear in the part of the word you have underlined.

What do you notice about the number of consonant letters and sounds?

3 Work in pairs and complete this table with words that begin with these consonant clusters. If no word in English begins with the cluster, write *X*. For example, the word *clock* begins with the consonant cluster /kl/; there is no word in English that begins with the consonant cluster /km/; the word *cry* begins with the consonant cluster /kr/.

The pictures may help you to complete some of the boxes.

	/l/	/m/	/r/
/k/	clock	X	cry
/d/			
/g/			
/p/			
/s/			
/t/			

4 In pairs, tell each other the words you have written. Underline any words you find difficult to say.

5 Compare answers with the rest of the class.

6 Look at this word chain.

blue
brush
cry
clock
slow
start
spin
play

Each word begins with a consonant cluster. *One* of the consonant sounds is the same as in the consonant cluster beginning the previous word. Go around the class and make similar word chains.

If you give a wrong word or can't think of a word, you are out of the chain. Don't repeat words.

Consonant clusters at the beginnings of words

 **1** Repeat these words. Pay special attention to the pronunciation of the underlined parts of the words.

A. blue
  black
  blood
  blanket
  blouse

B. bring
  bread
  bridge
  brother
  break

C. cloudy
  clean
  clock
  clothes
  clearly

D. cry
  cream
  cross
  Christmas
  crowd

E. quite
  quietly
  quicker
  quarter
  question

F. please
  place
  plenty
  played
  plastic

G. practice
  proud
  pronunciation
  pretty
  programs

2 Work in pairs. *Fifteen* of the words in **1** are hidden in the box below. Can you find them? Look across and down. Circle the words.

C	A	B	R	O	T	H	E	R	E
O	C	L	O	C	K	T	R	I	P
P	L	A	S	T	I	C	A	L	L
R	E	N	T	I	P	R	Q	E	A
A	A	K	E	C	L	O	U	D	Y
C	R	E	A	M	A	W	I	D	E
T	L	T	R	I	C	D	C	E	D
I	Y	O	B	R	E	A	K	A	P
C	E	Q	U	A	R	T	E	R	E
E	W	O	R	D	S	C	R	Y	N

3 Compare answers with the rest of the class.

4 Repeat these words. Pay special attention to the pronunciation of the underlined parts of the words.

H. sleepy
slowly
slim
slippery
slippers

I. start
stop
still
station
street

J. spend
speaking
sports
special
spring

K. try
trip
trains
trouble
trumpet

L. dress
drive
drop
drums
dream

M. three
through
throw
thrillers
throat

5 Complete these conversations with words from groups A to M.

How many tickets do you want?

Th___, pl___.

What did you buy at the mall?

A cl___ and some new sl___.

Should we take the bus?

No, let's dr___. It's qu____.

Where should we meet?

At the br____ by the st_____.

Oh, no, I missed it.

Don't worry. There are pl____ more tr___ tonight.

He can't understand my English.

Tr_____ sp_____ more sl _____.

What do you like best on TV?

Sp____ pr_____ and thr_____.

What instruments do you play?

The tr_____ and the dr___.

6 Work in pairs and say the conversations together.

More on consonant clusters at the beginnings of words

1 Listen to these sentences. each one contains a word from either box A or box B. Write the word you hear in the space.

A

clock	brought
grow	plane
drive	true
play	stay
spend	sport

B

lock	bought
go	pain
dive	two
pay	say
send	support

1. Is the ____clock____ broken?
2. They'll _____ much higher than that.
3. I learned to _____ last summer.
4. Should we _____ now or later?
5. How much money did you _____?
6. How many have you _____?
7. The _____ was terrible.
8. Are you sure it's _____?
9. Did you _____ two weeks or three?
10. He's been a good _____.

2 Work in pairs. Say the sentences in **1** to your partner. Complete them with a word either from box A or from box B. Your partner should try to decide which box the word is from.

3 Write the words in the box in the spaces next to the pictures on page 45.

skis	a frying pan	a plate	a clock	a ski suit	gloves
a scarf	a sleeping bag	a flashlight	a dress	a sweater	
flippers	slippers	a credit card	a swimsuit	bug spray	

Consonant clusters / Part 3

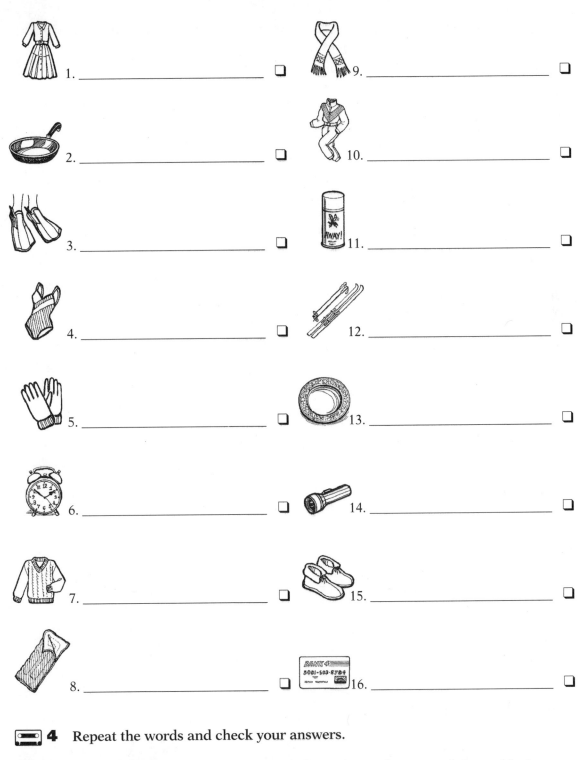

1. _____ ☐   9. _____ ☐

2. _____ ☐   10. _____ ☐

3. _____ ☐   11. _____ ☐

4. _____ ☐   12. _____ ☐

5. _____ ☐   13. _____ ☐

6. _____ ☐   14. _____ ☐

7. _____ ☐   15. _____ ☐

8. _____ ☐   16. _____ ☐

4 Repeat the words and check your answers.

5 Listen to Stephanie and Brandon talking about what to pack for a ski trip.
Put a check in the box next to each item in **3** that you hear mentioned.

6 Work in pairs. Have similar conversations about: (1) a camping trip and (2) a vacation at the beach. Use words from the box in **3**.

Here are some phrases to help you:

Should I take . . . ?   Yes, take that/those.
What about . . . ?   No, you won't need . . .
Do you think I'll need . . . ?

Don't forget to take . . .
You might need . . .
You might want to take . . .

Consonant clusters at the ends of words

 1 Listen to these words. Do you hear the word in column A or the one in column B? Put a check in the correct box.

	A		B				A		B	
1.	belt	❑	bell	❑		6.	card	❑	car	❑
2.	field	❑	feel	❑		7.	cold	❑	code	❑
3.	start	❑	star	❑		8.	needs	❑	knees	❑
4.	nights	❑	nice	❑		9.	fault	❑	fall	❑
5.	built	❑	bill	❑		10.	think	❑	thing	❑

2 Work in pairs. Your partner should say one of the words in each pair to you. Try to decide which one is being said. Take turns being listener and speaker.

 3 Many English words end in the sound /n/ followed by another consonant. Listen to these words. Some of them end in the *sounds* /ns/, /nt/, or /nd/. If they do, write them in the table. If they don't, leave them out.

/ns/	/nt/	/nd/
since	want	friend

 4 Listen again. Repeat the words and check your answers.

5 Complete these conversations with words from the table. Then work in pairs and say the conversations together.

6 Repeat these words. Pay particular attention to the consonant clusters at the ends of these words.

elephant	adult	pleased	belt	waist	wasp	child
fox	toast	yourself	pants	amused	beans	arm
shorts	hand	orange	depressed	parent	boyfriend	
shocked	milk	cold	chest			

7 Work in pairs. From the words in the box in **6** find some . . .

1. things you can eat or drink
2. things you can wear
3. parts of the body
4. animals
5. people
6. ways people feel

8 Compare answers with the rest of the class. For example:

There are four things you can eat or drink: . . .

Syllabic consonants; more on consonant clusters at the ends of words

A SYLLABIC CONSONANT occurs when a consonant forms a syllable by itself after another consonant, without any vowel sound between them. The sounds /l/ and /n/ are the most common syllabic consonants.

1 In the words here, syllabic /l/ or /n/ comes after a /t/ or /d/ sound. Try to say the /l/ or /n/ without moving your tongue away from the roof of your mouth after the /t/ or /d/.

Repeat these words.

bottle	middle	little	hospital	what'll
button	eaten	didn't	garden	mountain

2 Now repeat these words. These words are also usually pronounced without a vowel sound between the two consonant sounds at the end.

special	terrible	eleven	listen	haven't	chemical
happen	cousin	bicycle	chicken	final	

3 Work in pairs. Complete these conversations using words from the boxes in **1** and **2**.

1. A: Where's your _____?
   B: She's in the _____.
   A: What's the matter?
   B: She fell off her _____.

2. A: Have you _____?
   B: No, I _____.
   A: Would you like some _____?
   B: Just a _____.

3. A: Press that _____.
   B: This one in the _____?
   A: Yes.
   B: What'll _____?
   A: Just _____.

4. A: What's in this _____?
   B: A _____.
   A: What's it for?
   B: Something _____!

5. A: When's your math _____?
   B: At _____.
   A: How do you feel?
   B: _____.

4 Listen and check your answers.

 5 Listen again. Repeat the conversations one line at a time. Then say the conversations together with your partner.

6 Ask other students these questions and note how many people give each answer. Read the questions and the choices. For example:

Which of these subjects did you like best in school – science, economics, art, or politics?

Pay particular attention to the pronunciation of the underlined parts of the words.

1. Which of these subjects did you like best in school?

_____ scien<u>ce</u>   _____ ar<u>t</u>

_____ econo<u>m</u>ics   _____ poli<u>t</u>ics

2. Which of these colors do you like best?

_____ pur<u>pl</u>e   _____ ora<u>ng</u>e

_____ pi<u>nk</u>   _____ gol<u>d</u>

3. Which of these activities do you like to do best in your spare time?

_____ watch televi<u>si</u>on   _____ read boo<u>k</u>s

_____ play sp<u>or</u>ts   _____ gard<u>en</u>

4. Which of these jobs would you rather have?

_____ journali<u>st</u>   _____ arti<u>st</u>

_____ politi<u>cian</u>   _____ accoun<u>t</u>ant

5. Where would you rather work?

_____ in a hospi<u>t</u>al   _____ in a ba<u>nk</u>

_____ in a restauran<u>t</u>   _____ outdoo<u>rs</u>

6. Which of these countries would you rather go to for a vacation?

_____ Egy<u>pt</u>   _____ Thail<u>and</u>

_____ Fran<u>ce</u>   _____ Swe<u>den</u>

7. Which of these countries would you rather live in for the rest of your life?

_____ Egy<u>pt</u>   _____ Thail<u>and</u>

_____ Fran<u>ce</u>   _____ Swe<u>den</u>

7 Report your answers to the rest of the class. At the end, decide which subjects, colors, and so on were the most popular.

Groups of consonants in the middle of words; simplifying final consonant clusters

Groups of consonants in the middle of words

1 Work in pairs. Some of the words in the box have the *sounds* /ks/, /ky/, or /kw/ in the middle. If they do, write them in the table. If they don't, leave them out.

accident	occupation	require	record	equal	secure
success	taxi	vaccination	account	accent	particular
frequent	occur	calculator	liquid	exercise	

/ks/	/ky/	/kw/
accident	occupation	require

2 Listen and check your answers.

3 Listen again and repeat the words.

Fill in the spaces to make two rules about when to say the sounds /kw/ and /ks/.

1. The letters _____ are usually pronounced /kw/.

2. The letters *cc* are usually pronounced /ks/ before the letters _____ and _____.

4 Repeat these words. Pay attention to the underlined parts of the words.

taxi	painting	quietly	computers	practical
husband	opinions	airplane	boyfriend	raspberries
successful	appliances	frequently	afraid	equipment
scientist	onions	doctor	atlas	popular

5 Work in pairs. Choose words from the box in **4** to complete these sentences. The word you choose for each sentence should contain the sounds shown.

1. /kw/ We need some new ___equipment___ for the office.
2. /zb/ Have you met her new _____?
3. /nt/ It costs a lot nowadays to buy a good _____.
4. /tl/ Please play your records _____. The baby's asleep.
5. /ks/ I took a(n) _____ to the airport.
6. /fr/ Her _____ brings her flowers every day.
7. /ny/ I bought a pound of _____.
8. /kt/ She's studying to be a _____.
9. /py/ He's a very _____ actor.
10. /pl/ The price of the house did not include kitchen _____.

Simplifying final consonant clusters

6 Sometimes when more than two consonant sounds occur together at the end of a word, or across words, the middle consonant sound may be left out or almost left out. This happens especially to /t/, /θ/, /d/, and sometimes /k/.

Listen to these examples. Notice that grammatical endings like -s or -ed are *not* usually omitted.

jus\t one	nex\t February	Sen\d me a card.
las\t Saturday	two-fif\ths	I as\ked a question.

7 Listen and write the missing word in the spaces in these sentences.

1. It _____ too much.
2. He _____ weights.
3. He _____ her to marry him.
4. I _____ know yet.
5. I don't think she _____ him.
6. How much is this _____ bracelet?
7. Six _____.
8. Let's stop for some _____ food.
9. Thanks, anyway. I'm _____ looking.
10. Can you come _____ Saturday?

8 Listen again. Repeat the sentences and check your answers.

9 Work in pairs. Write the sentences from **7** in the spaces in these conversations. Then say the conversations together.

1. A: _Let's stop for some fast food._

   B: Let's go to a real restaurant for a change.

   A: _It costs too much._

   B: That's all you think about – money.

2. A: How does he stay in such great shape?

   B: _____

   A: Has he been doing that for long?

   B: _____

3. A: _____

   B: Two hundred dollars.

   A: _____

4. A: _____.

   B: I don't think she'll accept.

   A: Why not?

   B: _____

5. A: _____

   B: _____

   A: Please try.

PART 4 Stress and rhythm

Every language has its own rhythm. The patterns of stressed and unstressed syllables in words and sentences help create the rhythm of English. Knowing about English rhythm will help you understand others more easily and speak more clearly.

Unit 23 Syllables and stress

1 Words can be divided into SYLLABLES. For example:

farm	has one syllable
be-gin	has two syllables
com-put-er	has three syllables
in-tel-li-gent	has four syllables

How many syllables do these words have? Write your answers in the spaces.

1. furniture __3__
2. brought _____
3. blackboard _____
4. examination _____
5. remember _____

6. collect _____
7. anybody _____
8. please _____
9. police _____
10. grandmother _____

11. impossible _____
12. electricity _____
13. rabbit _____
14. directions _____
15. good-bye _____

2 Listen and check your answers.

3 Each word has one syllable that is STRESSED more than the others. In this book, the syllable that is stressed in a word will be marked by a big circle. The other syllables, which have less stress or are UNSTRESSED, will be marked by small circles. The circles will be placed over the vowel sound in each syllable.

Listen to these examples.

○◯
begin

○ ◯○
computer

○ ◯○○
intelligent

4 For each of the words in **1** that has more than one syllable, show the stressed syllable with a big circle and the other syllables with a small circle. For example:

○ ○ ○
furniture

5 Repeat the words and check your answers.

6 Here are the English names of some capital cities. How many syllables are there in each name? Show which syllable is stressed in English.

○ ○
Moscow __2__

Cairo _____

Tokyo _____

Madrid _____

Jakarta _____

Bogota _____

7 Repeat the names and check your answers.

8 *Two* words in each of these sentences have two syllables. Write ◯ ○ or ○ ◯ to show their stressed and **unstressed** syllables.

Patterns of stress in words

1 In each line, four of the words have the stress pattern shown, and one has a different pattern. This is the *odd one out*. Work in pairs and try to find the odd one out in each line.

1. ○ ○   above, chicken, prepare, guitar, correct

2. ○ ○   under, dirty, handsome, Japan, reason

3. ○ ○ ○   exciting, tomorrow, November, injection, president

4. ○ ○ ○   appointment, popular, yesterday, politics, sensitive

5. ○ ○ ○ ○ unemployment, competition, supermarket, information, immigration

2 Repeat the words and check your answers.

3 How many syllables do these words have? Write your answer in the space.

1. economics __4__

2. Chinese _____

3. August _____

4. accountant _____

5. Morocco _____

6. biology _____

7. photographer _____

8. chemistry _____

9. diplomat _____

10. Arabic _____

11. Italian ____

12. September ____

13. July ____

14. Russia ____

15. Germany ____

4 Repeat the words and check your answers.

5 Work in pairs. Use the words in **3** to complete these conversations. Choose a word that matches the stress shown. Then say the conversations together.

1. A: What does she do?
           ○ ○ ○

   B: She's a(n) _____.

2. A: When are you going on vacation?
             ○ ○

   B: In _____.

3. A: I really liked history in school.
            ○ ○ ○ ○

   B: My favorite subject was _____.

4. A: Do you speak Spanish?
           ○ ○ ○

   B: No, but I know some _____.

5. A: Where are you flying to?

   B: First to France and then on to
         ○ ○ ○

      _____.

Unit 25

More practice: stress in numbers; stress in noun compounds

Stress in numbers

 1 Listen to these sentences. Draw a circle around the number you hear.

1. 10:14	10:40		5. $1.18	$1.80
2. 15	50		6. $19.00	$90.00
3. 13	30		7. 1916	1960
4. 17	70			

2 If you are not sure whether someone has said "30" or "13," "40" or "14," and so on, you should ask the person to repeat. These conversations show you how.

Listen.

A: He'll be thirty tomorrow.

B: I'm sorry. Did you say thirty or thirteen?

A: Thirty.

A: She lives in apartment fourteen.

B: I'm sorry. Did you say forty or fourteen?

A: Fourteen.

Note that numbers ending in *-ty* (like *thirty* or *forty*) are stressed on the first syllable. Numbers ending in *-teen* (like *thirteen* or *fourteen*) are typically stressed on the last syllable when they are said on their own or at the end of a phrase or sentence.

3 Listen again. Repeat the conversations one line at a time.

4 Work in pairs to make similar conversations starting with these sentences.

1. Turn to page 17.
2. That will be $30, please.
3. To get to the theater, take bus number 80.
4. I'll see you at 3:15.

Stress in noun compounds

5 A NOUN COMPOUND occurs when two words come together to form a new noun. The new noun is sometimes written as one word and sometimes as two words, but it is used and pronounced as a single word, with one main stress, usually on the first word in the compound.

Listen to these noun compounds.

ice cream

airplane

living room

newspaper

blackboard

6 Listen to these phrases. Which contains a noun compound, the phrase in column A or the one in column B? Put a check in the correct box. Remember that a noun compound typically has strong stress only on the first part.

A		B	
1. a raincoat	☑	a wool coat	❏
2. a large office	❏	the post office	☑
3. a good driver	❏	a cab driver	❏
4. a long book	❏	a notebook	❏
5. a dining room	❏	a dirty room	❏
6. an office building	❏	a modern building	❏
7. a white house	❏	the White House	❏
8. a sleeping bag	❏	a sleeping child	❏

7 Mark the main stress in these noun compounds by using a large circle.

Shopping List	
paintbrush	toothpaste
alarm clock	measuring tape
shower curtain	dish towels
bookcase	cookbook
desk lamp	answering machine
orange juice	frying pan
tomato sauce	washing machine
can opener	garbage can
lightbulbs	salad dressing

8 Repeat the words and check your answers.

9 Jennifer and Jason are moving to a new house. They have made a list of things they need to buy, shown in **7**. Work in pairs and decide where they need to go to buy each thing. Choose from the stores in the box, or use your own ideas. Then report your decisions to the class.

> department store   hardware store   supermarket
> appliance store   drugstore   furniture store   bookstore

Note: The store names have typical noun compound stress.

10 What is a good place in your community to do the things below? Discuss this with your class. What's a good place to . . .

1. buy a birthday card?
2. get ice cream?
3. make photocopies?
4. get passport pictures?
5. get a money order?
6. buy a sleeping bag?
7. buy sunglasses?
8. buy a tape recorder?
9. get a haircut?

Unit 26 Pronouncing unstressed syllables

1 In the words in the boxes, the stressed syllables have a large circle over them.

  Listen to these pairs of words. Compare the way the underlined letters are pronounced.

A

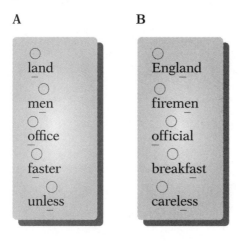

○ land
○ men
○ office
○ faster
○ unless

B

○ England
○ firemen
○ official
○ breakfast
○ careless

2 The underlined vowel in the words in box B is /ə/, often called *schwa*. In an unstressed syllable, the vowel is often pronounced as a very short /ə/. In the following words, the stressed syllable has a large circle over it, and vowels pronounced /ə/ are underlined.

  Repeat these words.

○ ○   ○ ○   ○ ○ ○   ○○ ○ ○   ○ ○ ○
about   famous   suggestion   photography   instrument

3 Work in pairs. Put a large circle over the syllable with the main stress, put a small circle over the unstressed syllables, and underline the vowels pronounced /ə/.

     ○ ○ ○
1. completely

5. excellent

9. success

2. jealous

6. machine

10. distance

3. apartment

7. woman

11. vanilla

4. biology

8. women

12. question

Part 4 / Stress and rhythm   **61**

4 Repeat the words and check your answers.

5 In these words, the underlined part is pronounced /ər/. This is the same sound practiced in Unit 8, but here it is *unstressed*.

 Repeat the words.

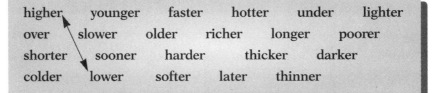

answer forget remember visitor dollar picture

6 Work in pairs. Say a word in the box. Your partner should find a word in the box that means the *opposite* of the word you say.

> higher younger faster hotter under lighter
> over slower older richer longer poorer
> shorter sooner harder thicker darker
> colder lower softer later thinner

7 Compare answers with the rest of the class. For example:

higher and lower

8 The last syllable in words that end in *-er, -or, -(i)an, -man,* and *-ant* is usually pronounced with /ə/.

 Repeat this list of jobs.

> doctor actor photographer
> teacher hairdresser optician
> electrician firefighter
> police officer flight attendant

9 Work with a partner. Read each pair of jobs and decide which worker you think earns more money. Then decide which job you think is more challenging.

1. A doctor or a police officer?

2. A teacher or a firefighter?

3. A photographer or an electrician?

4. A hairdresser or a flight attendant?

5. An actor or an optician?

10 Report your answers to the rest of the class.

Predicting stress in words

1 Word stress in English is complicated, but there are some simple rules that can be helpful. Write *N* for *noun*, *V* for *verb*, or *A* for *adjective* after these words.

carry _V_   famous _A_   daughter _N_   husband _____

forget _____   careful _____   modern _____   prefer _____

frighten _____   kitchen _____   friendly _____   doctor _____

2 Listen to the words in **1**. Put a large circle over the stressed syllable and a small circle over the unstressed syllable in each word.

3 Now complete these sentences with the words in the box to get some simple rules for *two-syllable words* in English.

> nouns   verbs   adjectives

Most _____ and _____ are stressed on the first syllable.
Some _____ are stressed on the first syllable, and others on
the second.

4 Many words in English have endings such as *-ion, -ity, -ic,* and *-ical*. These endings can help you figure out where the stress goes.

Listen to these words and put a large circle over the syllable that has the main stress.

     ○
1. decision   5. equality   9. magnetic   13. musical

2. suggestion   6. possibility   10. scientific   14. medical

3. institution   7. responsibility   11. enthusiastic   15. political

4. identification   8. personality   12. democratic   16. psychological

5 Now try these words. Work in pairs. Put a large circle over the syllable that has the main stress in each word.

1. invention
2. examination
3. ability
4. opportunity

5. electronic
6. romantic
7. practical
8. physical

6 Repeat the words and check your answers.

Complete this sentence to get a rule for words with these endings.

Words that end in *-ion, -ity, -ic,* and *-ical* usually have the main stress on the syllable _____ the ending.

7 Which of the adjectives in box A can be used to describe the nouns in box B?

Work in pairs. Discuss your answers with your partner and be ready to report back to the rest of the class. Report your answers like this:

You might say "a medical examination," but probably not "a medical personality."

A

romantic	medical
fantastic	electronic
scientific	enthusiastic
physical	political
musical	practical

B

question	suggestion
ability	discussion
invention	examination
personality	opportunity
composition	profession

8 Repeat these words and phrases.

generosity   punctuality   dependability   creativity   ambition
popularity   a good education   a pleasant personality   sincerity
curiosity   a sense of humor   sensitivity   patience
having the same opinions as you

9 Which three qualities in the box in **8** do you think are the most important in . . .

1. a friend?
2. a husband or wife?
3. a roommate?
4. an employee?
5. a teacher?

Work in small groups and compare your answers.

Rhythm

1 Some very common words in English have two pronunciations, sometimes called their STRONG and WEAK forms. The table shows how the strong and weak forms of the words *to, and,* and *for* are pronounced.

Listen.

Strong form	Weak form	
to /tu/	/tə/	I'm going to the mall.
and /ænd/	/ən/ or /n/	men and women; hot and cold
for /fɔr/	/fər/	Wait for me.

The weak forms of these words are much more commonly used than the strong forms. The strong forms are used only when the word has some special emphasis, or is said on its own or at the end of a phrase. Notice that weak forms usually contain unstressed /ə/. More practice of strong and weak forms is given in Part 7.

2 Read these sentences and decide which word – *to, and,* or *for* – might be missing from each one.

Listen to the sentences and write the word you hear.

1. What's _____ dinner?
2. I'll go _____ see.
3. I have nothing _____ say.
4. A hundred _____ forty.
5. I'm going _____ Florida.
6. I have _____ go.
7. It's _____ you.
8. Two _____ a dollar.
9. My mother _____ father.
10. I have a lot _____ do.
11. Not _____ long.
12. What's six _____ eight?

3 Listen again. Repeat the sentences and check your answers.

4 Which of these foods go together? Complete each phrase with a word from the box.

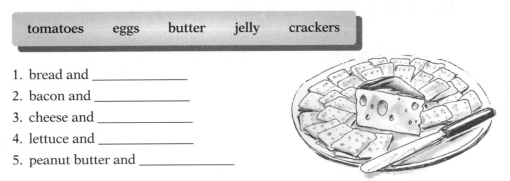

| tomatoes | eggs | butter | jelly | crackers |

1. bread and _____
2. bacon and _____
3. cheese and _____
4. lettuce and _____
5. peanut butter and _____

5 Repeat the phrases and check your answers. Use the weak form of *and*.

6 Think of more phrases that describe foods that go together. Then talk about what you are going to eat. One student should be A, and the others B, C, and so on. Go around the class. Each student repeats the list and adds a phrase. For example:

A: I'm really hungry. When I get home I'm going to have some bacon and eggs.
B: I'm going to have bacon and eggs, and bread and butter.
C: I'm going to have bacon and eggs, bread and butter, and lettuce and tomatoes.

When the list becomes too long to remember, start again.

More on rhythm

The pattern of stressed and unstressed syllables in a sentence helps create the rhythm of the sentence.

1 Repeat these sentences. Compare their rhythm.

1. Black or white?   2. Where are you from?   3. I go there a lot.

2 Listen to these sentences. Are they like 1, 2, or 3? Write the numbers in the spaces.

What did she say? _2_   Milk and bread. _____

I hope you can come. _____   I'll call the police. _____

What do we need? _____   She told me to rest. _____

Here's your change. _____   Out to lunch. _____

Where'd he go? _____   So do I. _____

Give me your purse. _____   Thanks very much. _____

3 Listen again. Repeat the sentences and check your answers.

4 Work in pairs. Draw lines to match the sentences. Make six two-line conversations. Then say the conversations together.

5 Work in pairs. One student should be A, and the other B.

Repeat each conversation one line at a time and then continue the dialog in the same way. Try to continue with the same rhythm as in the recording. The syllables to be stressed are in **bold** letters.

1. **When** should we **meet**?
   A: Should we **meet** on **Thurs**day?
   B: I **can't** on Thursday.
   A: Well, **how** about **Fri**day?
   B: I **can't** on Friday.
   A: Well, **how** about **Sat**urday?
   B: I **can't** on Saturday.
   A: Well, **how** about **Sun**day?

2. **When** should we **go**?
   A: Should we **go** in **Jan**uary?
   B: I **can't** in January.
   A: Well, **how** about **Feb**ruary?
   B: I **can't** in February.
   A: Well, **how** about **March**?

3. **What** should we **have** to **eat**?
   A: **Why** don't we have **fish**?
   B: I **don't like** fish.
   A: Well, **why** don't we have **chick**en?
   B: I **don't like** chicken.
   A: Well, **why** don't we have **beef**?

6 Work in pairs and write one more similar conversation called "Where should we go?" Practice it and then perform it for the rest of the class.

Rhythm and moving stress

1 Look at this picture of the students in an English language class. The students' occupations are written next to them. Find out their nationalities.

 Listen to the teacher talking about the class and write words from the box in the spaces.

> Chinese
> Polish
> Taiwanese
> Spanish
> Vietnamese
> Japanese
> Italian
> Colombian

dentist _____   journalist _____

diplomat _____   doctor _____

businessperson _____   actor _____

teacher _____   farmer _____

2 Listen to some of the words used by the teacher in the conversation. Put a large circle over the syllable that has the main stress.

Ja◯panese   Chinese   Taiwanese   Italian

Polish   Spanish   Colombian   Vietnamese

3 Listen again. Repeat the words and check your answers.

4 In some words, stress can move to a different syllable. This usually happens if another stressed syllable follows the word. For example:

He's Japa◯nese.   but   He's a Ja◯pan◯ese doctor.

Which of the other nationality words have this MOVING STRESS?

Listen and put a check next to the words with moving stress.

1. Japanese   ☑
2. Polish   ☐
3. Chinese   ☐
4. Spanish   ☐
5. Taiwanese   ☐
6. Colombian   ☐
7. Italian   ☐
8. Vietnamese   ☐

5 Many numbers also have this moving stress. Listen to this conversation. Notice how the *two* in *twenty-two* loses its stress when another stressed syllable follows it in a phrase.

A: Where does Jim live?

B: ◯Ma◦ple ◦Street.

A: What number does he live at?

B: ◯Twen◦ty-◯two.

A: So his address is . . .

B: ◯Twen◦ty-◦two ◯Ma◦ple ◦Street.

6 Listen again. Repeat the conversation one line at a time.

7 Work in pairs. Using these pictures, make questions and answers similar to those in **5**.

Stress and rhythm / Part 4

PART 5   *Sounds in connected speech*

It is sometimes difficult to understand speakers of English when they are talking at normal speed – which can sound very fast! One reason for this is that the pronunciation of some words is different when they are said on their own, or in slow, careful speech, from when they are used in CONNECTED SPEECH. *The units in Part 5 help you to understand and to practice connected speech in English.*

Unit 31   Slow speech and connected speech

Understanding sentences in connected speech

1 Listen and complete these sentences. They are said at normal speed.

1. ___*It's over*___ there.
2. _____ five _____.
3. _____ seven.
4. _____ do _____?
5. _____ soon _____.
6. _____ think _____.
7. _____ good.
8. _____ bad _____.
9. _____ said _____.
10. _____ do _____ tomorrow.

2 Listen to the sentences again. This time they are part of short conversations. If there were any sentences in **1** that you didn't understand, try to figure out what they are from the CONTEXT.

Understanding questions in connected speech

3 Read the answers to questions, shown in the balloons.

Listen to the questions and match them with the answers. Write the *number* of the question (for example, *1* or *5* or *8*) in the space under the correct picture.

I'm a doctor.

It's a box of chocolates.

About once a week.

a. _8_

b. _____

c. _____

Just a few minutes.

To a meeting.

I don't feel very well.

d. _____

e. _____

f. _____

Yes, we went to school together.

I'll have a cheeseburger.

g. _____

h. _____

4 Listen again. Write the questions in the balloons.

5 Listen to the conversations and repeat them one line at a time.

6 Work in pairs. Say the conversations together. Try to say them at the speed used in normal conversation.

Common words and phrases in connected speech

1 Some very common words have WEAK forms that are normally used in connected speech. (For more on weak forms, see Unit 28 and Part 7.) Read the sentences and decide what word might be missing from each one.

Listen and write the word you hear.

1. Two _____ three.
2. Call _____ ambulance.
3. On _____ off.
4. Saturday _____ Sunday.
5. Some _____ over here.

6. It's a container _____ ice cream.
7. _____ they coming?
8. Is that a picture _____ your sister?
9. He wants _____ computer.
10. Some _____ already paid.

2 Listen again. Repeat the sentences and check your answers.

3 This table shows how the words you wrote in **1** are usually pronounced. Why are there two pronunciations for *of*?

/ə/	a, of
/ər/	or, are
/əv/	of, have
/ən/	and, an

Note: The sound /ə/ is pronounced as in *ago* or *driver*.

4 Features of connected speech are sometimes shown in informal written English. This is often true for the words of popular songs. What do you think the underlined words in these lines from pop songs would be in normal written English? Write your answers in the spaces.

1. I don't <u>wanna</u> say that I've been unhappy with you. _____
2. All you've <u>gotta</u> do is call. _____
3. 'Cuz I'm happy just to dance with you. _____
4. I'm <u>gonna getcha</u> . . . . I'm <u>gonna meetcha</u>. _____
5. You <u>gotta</u> teach 'em 'bout freedom. _____

5 Listen to these conversations. Write the missing parts in the spaces. Use the normal written form of the words and phrases that you hear.

1. A: *I've got to go now.*

   B: _____

2. A: _____

   B: *I don't know.*

3. A: _____

   B: *No. When were they here?*

4. A: _____

   B: _____

5. A: _____

   B: _____

6. A: _____

   B: _____

6 Repeat the lines and check your answers.

7 Some words and phrases have BLENDED forms that are commonly used in connected speech. You do not have to use these pronunciations in your own speech, but you need to be able to understand them. For example, in some common expressions with *to*, the word *to* is blended with the word before it.

Listen to these examples:

got to ("gotta") – I've got to go now.
want to ("wanna") – What do you want to do?
going to ("gonna") – Are you going to go?
have to ("hafta") – I have to work late.
has to ("hasta") – She has to go to the doctor.

8 Practice making excuses. One student should be A, and the other students B, C, and so on. Say the conversation below, using your classmates' names. Then continue in the same way, adding a similar phrase when it is your turn to speak.

Use blended pronunciations of *want to, going to, have to,* and *has to*. What are some other excuses you can give?

A: We're going to see a movie tonight. Do you want to come?
B: I can't. I have to work late.
C: Mario has to work late and I have to go to the dentist.
D: Mario has to work late, Shu-fang has to go to the dentist, and I have to get up early tomorrow.

When the list becomes too long to remember, start again.

9 Work in pairs. Make plans to do something one evening. Decide on something to do (for example, go to the movies or go out for dinner) and find a time when you are both free. Then find as many other students as you can to come with you. Write the names of students you ask and note whether or not they can come. If they can't, write the reason they can't.

Here are some phrases to help you:

> We're going . . .
> Do you want to come?
> I'd like to, but I can't.
> I have to . . .

Report the results to the rest of the class.

Unit 33

Linking words together: consonant + vowel

In connected speech, words are usually linked together smoothly without a break between them. This unit provides practice in linking a word that ends in a consonant sound with a word that begins with a vowel sound.

1 Repeat these sentences. Make sure that you link the words together smoothly as shown.

1. An hour and a half.
2. It's upstairs.
3. He's an actor.
4. I found it.
5. Just a little.

6. Neither am I.
7. Both of us.
8. A while ago.
9. That's a lot of money.
10. This afternoon at four o'clock.

2 Work in pairs. Say the sentences to each other. Check that your partner is linking the words together.

3 Work in pairs. Choose five sentences from **1**. Write five two-line conversations. Each conversation should include one of the sentences you chose. For example:

A: *How long have you been waiting?*
B: An hour and a half.

4 Match the words on the left with the words on the right to describe what you see in the pictures.

a bottle
a pair
a box
a bunch
a set
a book
a deck
a roll

of flowers
of cards
of dishes
of earrings
of candy
of perfume
of film
of jokes

5 Repeat the phrases and check your answers. Make sure that you link the consonant sound at the end of the first part of the phrase with the vowel sound at the beginning of the word *of*.

6 Work in groups of three or four. Decide which of the things in **4** would be the best present for . . .

1. your mother
2. a girlfriend or wife
3. a teenager
4. a friend who is going on vacation
5. a friend who is in the hospital
6. someone who has invited you for dinner
7. a young couple getting married

You can give the same present to more than one person.

7 Work in pairs. Make a list of what you put on, take off, and so on. Use words from this box and try to think of more.

> the radio   the stove   an application   a fire   your coat
> a light   a car   the garbage   a bus   your clothes

1. You put on _____
2. You put out _____
3. You put away_____
4. You take off _____
5. You take out _____

6. You turn off_____
7. You turn up_____
8. You get on _____
9. You get in_____
10. You fill out_____

8 Report what you have written to the rest of the class. For example:

You put on your clothes.
You put out a fire.

Linking words together: consonant + consonant

This unit provides practice in linking a consonant sound at the end of a word with a different consonant sound at the beginning of the next word, as in *walk slowly*.

1 Match each word on the left with a word on the right to form a new word or phrase.

arrival	handed	truck	towel
drug	music	orange	juice
classical	time	dish	television
left	store	portable	driver

2 Repeat the phrases and compare them with your answers.

3 What other words can come before the words on the right in each box? Work in pairs to make three new words or phrases using some of the words on the right. Add words that end in a *consonant* sound. For example:

department store
pop music

4 Repeat these phrases and then listen to the conversation.

like them	think they're
that's very	it's true

A: Do you like them?
B: I think they're great.
A: That's very nice of you.
B: Really. It's true.

5 Repeat these phrases and then listen to the conversation.

is this	this correct	and this
this one	I'm not	not sure

A: Is this correct?
B: Those two are.
A: And this one?
B: I'm not sure.

6 Repeat these phrases and then listen to the conversation.

> last Friday   missed them
> they'll be   next March

A: When were they here?
B: Last Friday.
A: Oh, no. I missed them.
B: They'll be back next March.

7 Repeat these phrases and then listen to the conversation.

> was there   this morning
> Steve borrowed   have keys
> keys for   we'd better

A: It was there this morning.
B: Maybe Steve borrowed it.
A: He doesn't have keys for it.
B: Then we'd better call the police.

8 Match the conversations in **4** to **7** with these pictures. What are the people talking about in each conversation?

a. _____

b. _____

c. _____

d. _____

9 Work in pairs and say the conversations together.

More on linking words together with consonants

1 When the *same* consonant sound ends a word and starts the next word, as, for example, in a *right turn*, the consonant sound is usually pronounced only once, but slightly longer than usual.

Repeat the word in column 1, then repeat the word in column 2, and finally, repeat the two words together.

1	2	3
right	turn	We lost the game _____.
one	nothing	Is there _____ for the party?
black	car	The _____ called again.
enough	food	Make a _____ at the corner.
bad	dream	_____ on the couch.
more	rice	She was driving a _____.
let's	sit	Would you like _____?
same	man	A _____ woke me up.

2 Work in pairs. Write each phrase (for example, *right turn*) from columns 1 and 2 in the correct sentence in column 3. Then say the sentences to your partner.

3 When a consonant sound ends one word and a different consonant sound starts the next word, sometimes the pronunciation of the consonant at the end of the first word changes. This often happens in connected speech, especially when the consonants /t/, /d/, and /n/ are followed by the sounds /m/, /b/, /p/, /g/, or /k/.

Listen. Compare the words said on their own and in these sentences. Notice how the last consonant sound in the word changes.

clean – I have to clean͜ my apartment. need – We need͜ more milk.

don't – Don't͜ believe it. own – She has her own͜ car.

4 Repeat these phrases. Notice the change in the pronunciation of the consonant at the end of the first word.

1. on Monday
2. ten people
3. met Bob
4. went back
5. seven million

6. loud bang
7. quite boring
8. brown bag
9. television program
10. broken mirror

11. credit card
12. green car
13. in Canada
14. ran quickly
15. felt bad

5 Work in pairs. Write two sentences that include two or more of the phrases in **4**. For example:

On Monday, I watched a television program about computers, but it was quite boring and I fell asleep.

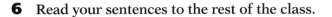
_____

_____

_____

6 Read your sentences to the rest of the class.

7 Sometimes two consonant sounds can be pronounced together as one different sound. This often happens in relaxed conversation when the consonant /t/, /d/, /s/, or /z/ at the end of a word is followed by /y/ at the beginning of the next word (especially in *you* or *your*).

Listen.

Don't forget your passport.
            tʃ
You won't need your jacket.
            dʒ

You'll miss your train.
            ʃ
Don't lose your camera.
            ʒ

8 Repeat each word, first on its own and then with the word *your*.

forget   need   miss   lose   put

9 Work in pairs. Your college-age son or daughter is about to leave for vacation. Give him or her some advice. Use the words in **8** (*forget, need, miss, lose, put*) plus *your*.

Here are some other words and phrases to help you:

> tickets   train   passport   gloves   jacket
> plane   camera   address book   bathing suit

> Don't forget your . . .
> You might need your . . .
> Put your . . . in a safe place.
> Don't put your . . . in your suitcase.
> Don't lose your . . .
> You'll need your . . .
> You won't need your . . .
> Hurry up, or you'll miss your . . .

Sounds that link words: /w/ and /y/

1 You will hear a conversation between Joe and Mary Ann. Listen to the conversation and answer the questions.

1. When is Brian's birthday?

   _____

2. What present do Joe and Mary Ann decide to get him?

   _____

3. When are they going to have a party?

   _____

2 Some of the words in the conversation are linked by a /w/ sound. Listen.

What about a new‿umbrella?   Yeah, let's do‿it Saturday.
             w   w

3 Some other words are linked by a /y/ sound. Listen.

. . . free‿on Saturday.   . . . Thursday‿evening?
        y   y

4 Repeat these sentences. The words marked are linked by a /w/ sound.

1. You know‿it's Brian's birthday.
2. Oh,‿I forgot all about it.
3. What about a new‿umbrella?
4. He should just throw‿it away.
5. It won't be too‿expensive.
6. How‿about Thursday?
7. He has an interview‿on Friday.
8. Yeah, let's do‿it Saturday.
9. You‿arrange the party.

5 Repeat these sentences. The words marked are linked by a /y/ sound.

1. It's Brian's birthday on Thursday.
   y

2. We should buy him a present.
   y

3. We really ought to have a
   y

   party or something for him.

4. Do you have any ideas?
   y

5. If we pay about $20, we could
   y

   get him something nice.

6. Why don't we invite a few friends?
   y

7. What about Thursday evening?
   y

8. More people will be free on Saturday.
   y

6 Look at these sentences. Will the words marked be linked by /w/ or /y/? Write *w* or *y* under the linking mark.

No, I didn't.   He must be at the office.
   w

Hi, Ann!   Go ahead.

There's no answer.   Did you see it?

Sunday afternoon.   When can you do it?

Can I try it?   Hi, how are you?

7 Repeat the sentences and check your answers.

8 Work in pairs. Draw arrows to match the sentences in **6**. Make five two-line conversations. Then say the conversations together.

Short sounds and disappearing /h/

1 In connected speech, the first syllable of words that begin with the unstressed sound /ə/ is often very short and may be difficult to hear.

Listen and compare these examples.

long – It's long.   along – It's along here.
way – I'm going this way.   away – I'm going away.

2 Listen to these conversations and write the words you hear in the spaces. Use the context to help you.

1. A: Where does she live?

   B: Just _____ the street.

2. A: Do you think I'm right?

   B: Yes, I _____ completely.

3. A: Can't you sleep?

   B: No, I've been _____ for hours.

4. A: When did you move here?

   B: Two years _____.

5. A: Don't you get lonely in that big house?

   B: No, I like living _____.

6. A: Is the bank near here?

   B: Yes. It's _____ five minutes _____.

7. A: Can I speak to David?

   B: Sorry, he's _____ right now.

8. A: Have you seen my keys?

   B: Yes, they're _____ here somewhere.

3 The sound /h/ at the beginning of some words is very short or may not be pronounced at all.

Listen to these examples.

Does he like it?   What's her name?

4 Listen to these short conversations. The /h/ sounds are underlined. Draw a line through them if they are very short or not pronounced.

1. A: Have they found ~~h~~im?
   B: Who?
   A: The man ~~who~~ robbed your house.

2. A: Did he tell her what happened?
   B: He did, but she didn't believe him.

3. A: How's Henry these days?
   B: Didn't you hear about his heart attack?

4. A: Did you call him?
   B: He wasn't home. He must have left already.

5. A: It says here that the President's coming.
   B: Where's he going to be?
   A: Here.
   B: Oh, I hope we'll be able to see him.

6. A: What are you children fighting about?
   B: It's MY book.
   C: HIS book's over THERE.
   B: HER book's over there. This one's mine!

5 Find the words in **4** that are sometimes pronounced with the sound /h/ and sometimes without. When *is* /h/ pronounced in these words?

6 Work in pairs and say the conversations together. When the sound /h/ is dropped, make sure that you link the word to the word before it. For example:

Have they found ~~h~~im?

In Part 6, you will learn about the intonation, or melody, of English. Three things are important: whether a word is prominent or not, whether the voice rises or falls in pitch, and where this rise or fall begins.

Unit 38   Prominent words

In Part 4, you learned about stress in words. In this unit, you will learn about stress in sentences, called PROMINENCE. Words that are prominent are usually the words that the speaker thinks are the most important in the sentence.

1 In these sentences, one word is prominent, or stands out from the rest. Listen and circle the prominent word in each sentence.

1. (Thank) you.   6. He's my uncle.
2. I'm tired.   7. He's an accountant.
3. Chris did.   8. It's raining again.
4. It's getting late.   9. She's in the living room.
5. I'm sure she will.   10. She told me about it.

2 Listen again. Repeat the sentences.

3 Match the answers in **1** with these sentences. In this exercise, prominent words are written in **CAPITAL LETTERS**. Note that in words with more than one syllable, even though the whole word is written in capital letters, only one syllable is actually prominent.

a. WHO cooked DINNER? _3_   f. Is THAT your FATHER? _____
b. This is for YOU. _____   g. Are you FEELING OK? _____
c. WHAT does DAN do? _____   h. What TIME is it? _____
d. WHAT'S the WEATHER like? _____ i. WHERE'S JESSICA? _____
e. DONNA BOUGHT a HOUSE. _____   j. Do you THINK she'll LIKE it? _____

4 Listen to the conversations and check your answers.

5 Work in pairs and say the conversations together. Make the words you circled in **1** and the words shown in capital letters in **3** prominent.

6 *Any* word can be prominent if the speaker thinks it is important in a sentence, but some kinds of words are much more likely to be prominent than others. The words that give the most information are most likely to be prominent. Look at these sentences from **1** and **3** again. The prominent words are shown in capital letters here.

> What TIME is it?
> I'm TIRED.
> She TOLD me about it.
> He's my UNCLE.
> Do you THINK she'll LIKE it?
> DONNA BOUGHT a HOUSE.

Notice the kinds of words that are prominent, and complete the rules below with the words from the box on the right.

1. Content words – for example, nouns (like *time*), verbs (like *told*), and adjectives (like *tired*) – are typically _____.

2. Grammar words – for example, pronouns (like *she*), articles (like *a*), and prepositions (like *about*) – are typically _____.

> prominent
> not prominent

7 Match words in box A with words in box B. How many dishes are there that you might find in a restaurant? Where are these foods from? Decide if a dish is Indian, Mexican, Chinese, Japanese, or American and add it to the menu on the next page.

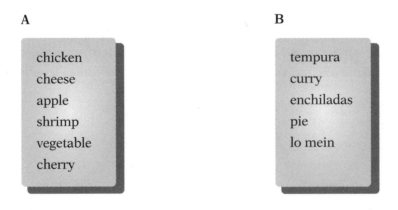

A

> chicken
> cheese
> apple
> shrimp
> vegetable
> cherry

B

> tempura
> curry
> enchiladas
> pie
> lo mein

INTERNATIONAL HOUSE

"We give you the world on a platter."

◇◇◇◇
INDIAN SPECIALTIES
chicken curry

◇◇◇◇
CHINESE SPECIALTIES

◇◇◇◇
MEXICAN SPECIALTIES

◇◇◇◇
JAPANESE SPECIALTIES

◇◇◇◇
AMERICAN SELECTIONS
cherry pie

8 Repeat the names of some of the dishes. Make both words prominent.

9 In the sentences shown in the pictures, the prominent words are in capital letters. Notice that the repeated word is not prominent. This often happens with repeated words.

Listen and repeat the sentences.

10 Listen to this conversation. Then work in groups of three to make similar conversations.

Repeated words and prominence

1 Listen to these conversations. The prominent words are written in capital letters. Notice what happens to the word from the question that is repeated in the answer.

   1. A: She LOOKS kind of TIRED, DOESN'T she?
      B: YES, VERY tired.

   2. A: Are you FREE on SUNDAY?
      B: What TIME on Sunday?

Listen again to what A says. When you hear the tone, say B's part. Then listen and repeat what B says.

Continue in the same way, taking B's part.

   3. A: Do you have any in dark blue?
      B: No, sorry, only light blue.

   4. A: Are you feeling better?
      B: Oh, yes. Much better.

   5. A: Should we meet at one?
      B: Can we make it a quarter after one?

   6. A: And the winning number is 5-4-9.
      B: That's my number.

   7. A: Is he an artist?
      B: Actually, a very good artist.

   8. A: Did you say Tom was in the front yard?
      B: No, the backyard.

2 Work in groups of three. Say the conversations in **1**. One student should take A's part, one should take B's part, and the third student should *monitor* what B says. Check particularly that the repeated word is not made prominent.

3 Listen. Which of the pictures on page 93 (a, b, or c) is being described? Circle the answer.

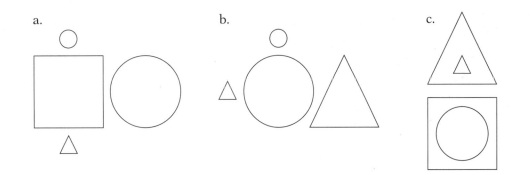

a.   b.   c.

4 Listen to these sentences. Underline the words in the boxes that are prominent.

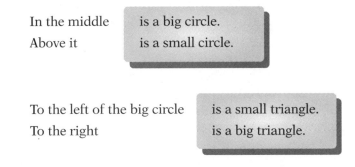

| In the middle | is a big circle. |
| Above it | is a small circle. |

| To the left of the big circle | is a small triangle. |
| To the right | is a big triangle. |

What can you say about the repeated words?

5 Take a piece of paper and draw a picture similar to the pictures in **3**. It should be made up of big and small circles, squares, and triangles, and should include four or five shapes altogether. Don't let your partner see what you have drawn.

Then describe the picture to your partner. Your partner should try to draw what you describe on a separate piece of paper. When you have finished, compare your picture and your partner's drawing. Discuss any differences. Then repeat the activity, with your partner drawing a picture and describing it to you.

Here are some words and phrases to help you:

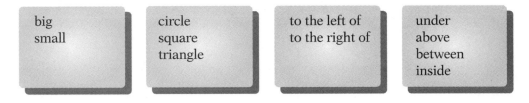

| big
small | circle
square
triangle | to the left of
to the right of | under
above
between
inside |

More on prominent and nonprominent words

1 Complete the conversations with words from the box.

| us | them | there | one | him | her | he |

1. A: Do you want some grapes?
   B: No, thanks, I don't like _____.

2. A: Does Kathy know the answer?
   B: I'll ask _____.

3. A: What do you think of California?
   B: I've never been _____.

4. A: This is my son, Nicholas.
   B: How old is _____?
   A: Three.

5. A: Wasn't that Peter?
   B: Sorry, I didn't see _____.

6. A: I'm living in Boston now.
   B: Do you like it _____?

7. A: Does she live on this street?
   B: No, it's the next _____.

8. A: Can I reserve a table for tonight?
   B: Certainly. For how many people?
   A: There'll be three of _____.

2 Listen to the conversations and check your answers.

Notice that the words you have written are not prominent. Why do you think this is?

3 Work in pairs. Say the conversations. Make sure that the words you have written are not prominent.

4 At the end of a sentence, certain expressions of time are typically not prominent. These include words and phrases like *yesterday, today, tomorrow, soon, now, this morning,* and *last night*.

Listen. The expressions of time are underlined, and prominent words are written in capital letters.

A: What's NEW?
B: I'm MOVING tomorrow.

A: I SPOKE to ANNA this morning.
B: Oh, REALLY? How IS she?

A: HOW did you get SUNBURNED?
B: I WENT to the BEACH yesterday.

These time expressions can be prominent, however, if the speaker thinks that they are important in a sentence – for example, to focus on when something happened or will happen, to answer a question about time, or for contrast.

Listen again.

A: I HEAR you FOUND a NEW APARTMENT.
B: YES. I'm MOVING TOMORROW.

A: Have you SPOKEN to ANNA lately?
B: YES. I SPOKE to her this MORNING.

A: Do you WANT to go to the BEACH today?
B: NOT REALLY. I WENT to the beach YESTERDAY.

5 Work in pairs. The time expression in the first line of each conversation is not prominent. Try to decide if the other time expression(s) in each conversation would be prominent. Put a check (✓) in the space if the expression would be prominent or a dash (–) if it would not be prominent.

1. A: I have to leave soon.

   B: Me, too. I have to get up early tomorrow.   —

2. A: I'm living in Boston now.

   B: Have you been living there long?

   A: No. I moved there last week.   ✓

3. A: What's for dinner tonight?

   B: Chicken.

   A: But we had chicken last night.   _____

4. A: Are you going away this weekend?

   B: Maybe. I'm not sure yet.   _____

5. A: Is it supposed to snow tonight?

   B: I don't know. I didn't hear a weather forecast today. _____

6. A: I'm going back to school tomorrow.

   B: I thought classes started next week.   _____

   A: No, they start tomorrow.   _____

7. A: I didn't see you last week. Were you away?

   B: Yes. I just got back yesterday. _____

8. A: I hear you're going to Florida soon.

   B: Yes, I'm leaving tomorrow. _____

6 Listen and check your answers. Then say the conversations together with your partner.

7 It is Saturday, and Melissa and Paul are talking about what to do. Listen. Prominent words are in capital letters.

Notice that Paul puts prominence on both what he did and when he did it. He puts prominence on the time expression to show why he doesn't want to do the same activity *now*.

8 Listen again. Repeat the conversations one line at a time.

9 Work in pairs. Make similar conversations using these phrases. Follow the same pattern used in **7**.

1. visit your sister   saw Lynn/Wednesday
2. go to the theater   saw a play/Tuesday
3. go for a walk   went to the park/this morning
4. watch TV   watched TV/this afternoon

Falling and rising intonation

1 In FALLING INTONATION in English, the voice *jumps up* on the stressed syllable of the last prominent word in the sentence, and then *falls* after that. If this syllable is at the very end, the voice jumps up and falls on the same syllable.

Listen to these examples. Prominent words are in capital letters. Notice how the voice falls at the end.

She's from CHICAGO.   It's MINE.   HELP YOURSELF.

I MET him at a PARTY.   NOBODY TOLD him.   WHERE do you LIVE?

Now listen to these examples. Notice how the voice *rises* at the end.

Are they HERE yet?   Is this YOURS?   READY?

Would you LIKE one?   Nobody TOLD him?   MAYBE.

2 Listen to these short sentences. The prominent words are in capital letters. Put a down-pointing arrow (↘) in the space if the voice jumps up and then falls at the end. Put an up-pointing arrow (↗) if the voice rises.

1. THANKS ___↘___
2. My KEY ___↗___
3. CREAM _____
4. There's some CAKE left _____
5. EIGHTY DOLLARS _____
6. I'm HUNGRY _____
7. Can't you GUESS _____
8. On the TABLE _____

9. HOW much IS it _____
10. I DRINK it BLACK _____
11. Are you going to BUY it _____
12. In the KITCHEN _____
13. WHAT _____
14. I FOUND something _____
15. COFFEE _____
16. It's TOO EXPENSIVE _____

3 Listen again. Repeat the sentences and check your answers.

4 Work in pairs. Arrange the sentences in **2** into four 4-line conversations. Use the intonation to help you. Write the numbers of the sentences in the correct order in the spaces.

1. A: 6
   B: 4
   A: _____
   B: 8

2. A: 11
   B: _____
   A: _____
   B: 5

3. A: _____
   B: 13
   A: _____
   B: 2

4. A: 15
   B: _____
   A: _____
   B: _____

5 Listen to the conversations and check your answers. Then work in pairs and say the conversations together.

Focus on falling intonation

6 Listen to this conversation.

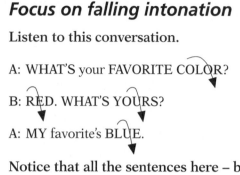

A: WHAT'S your FAVORITE COLOR?

B: RED. WHAT'S YOURS?

A: MY favorite's BLUE.

Notice that all the sentences here – both questions and answers – have falling intonation. Questions that ask for new information and statements that give information often have falling intonation. (Questions that ask for new information begin with a question word such as *what, when, where, how,* or *who.*)

7 Work in pairs and talk about the things in the box. Use this pattern.

A: WHAT'S your FAVORITE _____?

B: _____. WHAT'S YOURS?

A: MY favorite's _____.

color	time of year	food	drink
city	restaurant	TV show	sport

8 Work in pairs. On a small piece of paper, write a question beginning with *who, what, when, where,* or *how many.* On another small piece of paper, write the answer to that question. The question should ask about an item of general (not personal) knowledge, and the answer should be complete. For example:

What's the capital of Colombia?   The capital of Colombia is Bogota.
Who invented the telephone?   Alexander Graham Bell invented
                                                                the telephone.
How many legs does a spider have?   A spider has eight legs.

Put all the pieces of paper in a box and mix them up. Each student in the class should then take one of the slips of paper. Students should try to match questions and answers: A student who has a slip of paper with a question written on it tries to find the person who has the answer, and a student with an answer tries to find the person with the question.

Focus on rising intonation

 9 Repeat these questions.

Are you TIRED?

Are you READY?

Should I CLOSE the WINDOW?

Have YOU seen my KEYS?

Could I borrow a DOLLAR?

Wasn't that a GREAT MOVIE?

Notice that all these questions are said with rising intonation on the recording. Questions that can be answered "yes" or "no" often have rising intonation in North American English.

10 Work in pairs. One student should be A, and the other B. Student A should ask one of the questions in **9**. Student B should answer with one of the questions below. Take turns being A and B. Practice saying all the questions with rising intonation.

Do you need it now?
Do I look tired?
Did you lose them again?

Are you cold?
Did you really like it?
Is it time to leave already?

11 Repeat the conversations and check your answers.

More on falling and rising intonation

Asking someone to repeat

1 Rising intonation is often used to ask someone to repeat what he or she said.

 Listen to these examples.

What did you say?

Say that again?

Excuse me?

2 You can use rising intonation in questions beginning with a question word (such as *when, where,* or *who*) to ask about information you did not hear or understand.

Listen to these conversations. Notice the difference in intonation in the questions. Prominent words in the questions are in capital letters.

A: I'm going to China in the fall.

(asks for repetition) B: WHEN are you going?

A: In the fall.

A: I'm going to China in the fall.

B: WHEN are you GOING? *(asks for new information)*

A: In October.

3 Listen to the conversations again and repeat B's questions.

4 Listen to the intonation of the question in each of these short conversations and try to decide which answer should follow it. Put a check in the correct box.

1. A: I'm going to California next week.
   B: Where?
   A: ☑ California.
   ☐ San Francisco.

2. A: We're moving to New York next month.

   B: When are you moving?

   A: ❏ Next month.

   ☑ On the fifteenth.

3. A: I bought that rug in Mexico.

   B: Where?

   A: ❏ In Mexico.

   ❏ In Mérida, at an outdoor market.

4. A: I tried to call you last night.

   B: When?

   A: ❏ Last night.

   ❏ Around nine o'clock.

5. A: Richard left a present for you.

   B: What?

   A: ❏ I said, Richard left a present for you.

   ❏ I don't know. It's in a box.

6. A: My mother works in an office.

   B: What does she do?

   A: ❏ She works in an office.

   ❏ She's a receptionist.

7. A: I have an appointment on Tuesday.

   B: When is your appointment?

   A: ❏ On Tuesday.

   ❏ Eleven o'clock.

8. A: Someone I work with gave me this cassette.

   B: Who?

   A: ❏ Someone I work with.

   ❏ Linda Novak.

5 Work in groups of three to practice the short conversations in **4**. One student should take A's part, one student should take B's part, and the third student should *monitor* the questions and answers. Student B can use either rising or falling intonation in the questions. Student A should give the correct response, depending on which intonation B used. Take turns being A, B, and the monitor.

Giving choices

6 Michael is asking Nora to buy some things at the supermarket. Notice how Nora's voice rises on the first choice and falls on the second choice in her question.

Listen.

Michael: Can you get some cornflakes?

Nora: Do you want a large or small box?

Michael: A small one.

7 Listen again. Repeat the conversation one line at a time. Prominent words are in capital letters. Notice that words are prominent when there is a choice or a contrast.

Can you get some CORNFLAKES? —————— *Cornflakes – not coffee or yogurt or bread, etc.*

Do you want a LARGE or SMALL box? —————— *Not prominent because there is*
Large,   *Small,*   *no choice; you normally buy*
not small   *not large*   *cornflakes in a box*

A SMALL one.
Small, not large

8 Work in pairs and make similar conversations. For example:

A: Can you get some bread?
B: Do you want a large or small loaf?
A: A large one.

Use these words to help you, or think of other words you could use.

bottle	bunch	box		
container	can	loaf	jar

grapes	beans	detergent
jam	orange juice	bananas
bread	coffee	yogurt

Leaving things open

In Units 41 and 42, you practiced falling intonation (↘) and simple rising intonation (↗). Another common intonation in English first jumps up and falls, like the falling intonation practiced earlier, but then rises slightly. This intonation is called FALLING-RISING INTONATION (↘↗). It has many of the same uses as rising intonation.

Falling intonation on a statement, especially falling to a low note, suggests completeness or certainty. You have seen this use in statements that give information. Rising intonation on a statement (either simple rising or falling-rising) usually suggests incompleteness – that something more could, should, or will be said by either the speaker or the listener. It can also suggest uncertainty.

1 Because intonation that rises at the end (either simple rising or falling-rising intonation) gives a feeling of incompleteness, it is often used in the first part of a sentence.

Listen to these examples.

Turn left here and then go straight.

After we eat we could go and see Alison.

If I have to work late, I'll call you.

2 Listen to these sentence halves. (Capital letters and punctuation are not shown.) If you hear the first part of a sentence, write *A*. If you hear the end of a sentence, write *B*.

1. but you can't make him drink __B__
2. don't count your chickens __A__
3. you can lead a horse to water _____
4. get out of the kitchen _____
5. before they're hatched _____
6. if you can't stand the heat _____
7. do as the Romans do _____
8. it's how you play the game _____
9. when in Rome _____
10. it isn't whether you win or lose _____

3 Work in pairs. Each line in **2** is half of a common English saying. Match the A and B halves to form these sayings. For example:

You can lead a horse to water, but you can't make him drink.

Do you have sayings similar to any of these in your native language? If you do, try to write them down in English.

4 Compare answers with the rest of the class.

5 Sometimes people use the same kinds of "incomplete" intonation at the end of a sentence. For example, you can end a list of items with rising intonation to show that the list is not complete. Or you can end a sentence by adding a slight rise after a fall (falling-rising intonation) to show that there is something you are not saying.

A rise at the end leaves the situation open. A fall to a low note sounds more final, or closed.

Listen to these sentences. Do they sound open (O) or closed (C)? Write *O* or *C* in the space.

1. We need BREAD and MILK and BANANAS   _C_
2. He DRAWS well   _O_
3. I LIKE her SISTER   _____
4. The RESTAURANT isn't on EIGHTH Street   _____
5. We went to SPAIN and PORTUGAL and FRANCE   _____
6. It's POSSIBLE   _____
7. I'd LIKE to SEE it   _____
8. I THOUGHT you would   _____
9. I TOLD you so   _____
10. He SEEMS nice   _____

6 Work in pairs. Choose any three of the sentences in **5**. Imagine them as open sentences, even if they were not said that way on the recording. What could the speaker be leaving out? How could these sentences be completed? For example:

We need bread and milk and bananas *and onions.*
I'd like to see it, *but I don't have time.*

Compare completed sentences with the rest of the class. When you say your sentence, remember to make your voice fall to a low note at the end to show that you are finished.

7 Listen to these short conversations. Concentrate particularly on what B says in each. The first intonation that B uses is shown with an arrow. Is the second intonation B uses the same (S) or different (D)? Write *S* or *D* in the space.

1. A: Should we go for a drive?
   B: YES ↘ – I'd LOVE to. ↘   _S_

2. A: Can you come on Monday?
   B: YES ↘ – I THINK so.   _____

3. A: Do you mind if I open the window?
   B: NO ↘ – not REALLY.   _____

4. A: Are you going away this summer?
   B: MAYBE ↘ – I don't KNOW yet.   _____

5. A: John and Emily are getting married!
   B: REALLY ↗ – I THOUGHT they would.   _____

6. A: When are you going to the beach?
   B: On SUNDAY ↘ – if the WEATHER'S good.   _____

8 Listen again and decide what the second intonation is that B uses in each sentence. Draw arrows to show whether the intonation is falling, rising, or falling-rising.

9 Work in pairs and say the short conversations together. The student taking A's part should check that B is using the correct intonations. Take turns being A and B.

Unit 44 Focus words

1 The rise or fall in intonation begins on the most prominent word in the sentence – the word that the speaker sees as the most important. At the beginning of a conversation, this is *typically* the last noun or other content word (verb, adjective, or adverb) in the sentence.

Listen to these examples.

Do you HAVE the TICKETS?

MAYBE we should CALL her.

Do you PLAY the PIANO?

But as the conversation continues, the focus of information changes.

Listen.

A: Do you HAVE the TICKETS? B: I thought YOU took them.

A: MAYBE we should CALL her. B: I asked MIGUEL to call her.

A: Do you PLAY the PIANO? B: I USED to play.

2 Listen to these sentences and circle the FOCUS WORD – the word on which the fall or rise begins – in each.

a. It's on (top) of the bookcase. e. At five after one.
b. With milk, please. f. I finished it.
c. At five after one. g. It's on top of the bookcase.
d. I finished it. h. With milk, please.

3 Listen again. Repeat the sentences and check your answers.

4 Work in pairs and decide which of the sentences in **2** would be the best response to these sentences. Write the correct letter in the space.

1. A: Did you want your coffee without milk? B: _h_
2. A: See you at ten after one. B: ____

3. A: Where's the newspaper?   B: _____

4. A: Did you want coffee with cream?   B: _____

5. A: What happened to the cheese?   B: _____

6. A: I thought I put the newspaper in the bookcase.   B. _____

7. A: See you at five to one.   B: _____

8. A: Who finished the cheese?   B: _____

5 Listen and check your answers. Then say the short conversations together with your partner.

6 Look at these conversations. In some of the sentences, the focus word is circled. Decide which word you think would be the focus word in each of the other sentences. Circle it.

1. A: Can I (help) you?
   B: I'm looking for a coat.
   A: They're on the (second) floor.
   B: Thank you.

2. A: What do you (think)?
   B: I don't like the color.
   A: I thought you (liked) red.
   B: I prefer blue.

3. A: Should we eat (here)?
   B: Let's sit over there.
   A: Under (that) tree?
   B: The other one.

4. A: Can I speak to Rick?
   B: There's no (Rick) here.
   A: Is this 549-6098?
   B: No, this is 549-6078.

7 Listen and check your answers.

8 Listen again. Repeat the conversations one line at a time. Then work in pairs and say the conversations together.

9 Work in pairs. Look at the bus schedule. Ask questions that include *wrong* information. Your partner should correct you, and should put the focus on the new information – the information that is correct.

Listen to these examples. The focus word is circled.

DEPARTURES		
		Gate
Washington	9:00	29
Philadelphia	8:55	33
Boston	9:30	25
Hartford	9:55	35
Atlantic City	10:30	23

A: Does the bus to Philadelphia leave from gate 2(3)?

B: No, it leaves from gate (3)3.

A: Is there a bus to Hartford at 9:4(5)?

B: No, there's one at 9:(5)5.

Unit 45 Predicting intonation

1 In some of the lines in these conversations, the intonation is shown. Predict what it is likely to be in the other lines. Draw arrows starting at the FOCUS WORD. The focus word is shown in capital letters.

1. A: It was EXPENSIVE.

   B: How MUCH?

   A: Two thousand DOLLARS.

   B: HOW much?

2. A: What's on TV tonight?

   B: A HORROR film.

   A: Is it GOOD?

   B: I've HEARD it is.

3. A: Where's LUCY?

   B: She went HOME.

   A: She LEFT?

   B: About an HOUR ago.

4. A: Is it still RAINING?

   B: I THINK so.

   A: HARD?

   B: Not VERY hard.

2 Listen and check your answers.

If your answers were different, discuss the differences. Sometimes more than one intonation may be possible.

▭ 3 Listen again. Repeat the conversations one line at a time. Then work in pairs and say the conversations together.

▭ 4 Repeat these sentences with the intonation shown.

1. I ALWAYS have lunch there.

2. Should we go TONIGHT?

3. When are you GOING?

4. WHEN are you going?

5. I'd LIKE to.

6. I'd LIKE to.

5 Work in pairs and write six short conversations. Each conversation should include one of the sentences in **4** with the intonation shown. For example:

A: Should we have lunch?

B: OK. Let's go to the snack bar.

A: Why there?

B: I ALWAYS have lunch there.

6 Perform your conversations for the rest of the class.

Weak and strong forms; short and long forms

Weak and strong forms of *you* and the verbs *do, does,* and *can*

1 Many common grammar words in English have two pronunciations, a STRONG FORM and a WEAK FORM.

🔲 Listen. You will hear the *strong* forms of these words.

> does   you   do   can

🔲 Listen again. You will hear short sentences with the *weak* forms of the same words.

Where does he live?   See you later.   How do they know?   We can try.

In connected speech, weak forms are usually used. The strong form is used only if the word is *stressed*, for example to give it special emphasis or when the word is at the end of a phrase.

2 All the *weak* forms of the words you will practice in this unit contain the *unstressed* sound /ə/.

🔲 Listen again. Repeat the sentences from **1**.

🔲 **3** Repeat these questions. Pronounce the verbs *do, does,* and *can* and the word *you* with their weak forms.

1. Do you like it?
2. Can we go now?
3. Does he live here?
4. Can I take two?
5. Does it hurt?
6. When do you go back?
7. Why does she want to leave?
8. Where can we see one?
9. How do you feel now?

4 Work in pairs. Match each question from **3** with one of the answers below. Then say the short conversations together.

No, next door. _3_   In a zoo. _____   Yes, of course. _____

A little later. _____   Much better. _____   Tomorrow. _____

She's tired. _____   Not really. _____   Yes, very much. _____

Short and long forms of negative verbs

5 The NEGATIVE forms of the verbs *do*, *does*, and *can* have two forms, a SHORT form (or contraction) and a LONG form. They are written like this:

Short form	don't	doesn't	can't
Long form	do not	does not	cannot (*or* can not)

Repeat the short forms.

The short form is normally used in speaking and is sometimes used in writing, especially writing in an informal style.

6 Work in pairs. One partner should ask the questions below. Use the *weak* forms of the verbs and of the word *you*.

The other partner should give short answers like the ones in the box. In negative answers, use the *short* form (contraction). In positive answers, use the *strong* form because the verb is at the end of the sentence. The partner asking the question should write *Yes* or *No* in the spaces.

> Yes, I do.   No, I don't.
> Yes, I can.   No, I can't.

1. Do you have a driver's license?   _____

2. Can you speak French?   _____

3. Do you play any musical instruments?   _____

4. Can you draw well?   _____

5. Do you smoke?   _____

6. Can you stand on your head?   _____

7. Do you like cheese?   _____

8. Can you swim well?   _____

7 Report back to the class only the *negative* answers. For example:

1. Do you have a driver's license?   _No_ _Maria doesn't have a driver's license._
2. Can you speak French?   _Yes_ –
3. Do you play any musical instruments? _Yes_ –
4. Can you draw well?   _No_ _Maria can't draw well._

Can *and* can't

8 In connected speech, the word *can* is usually pronounced with its weak form and has the unstressed vowel /ə/. The negative form *can't* always has the vowel /æ/.

Listen to these sentences. Write whether you hear *can* or *can't*.

1. _can_   3. _____   5. _____   7. _____
2. _____   4. _____   6. _____   8. _____

9 Work in pairs. Talk about the activities in the box or other activities you can think of. Take turns talking about what you *can* and *can't* do. One partner should make statements, and the other partner should respond. For example:

A: I can cook.
B: So can I./Oh, I can't.

A: I can't cook.
B: Neither can I./Oh, I can.

Make a note of the things you have in common – the things that both of you *can* or *can't* do.

Remember to use the weak form of *can*, except at the end of a sentence.

cook	read music	play the piano	drive
swim	ski whistle	play chess	sail a boat
fly a plane	ride a horse	write with either hand	

10 Report to the class on the things you have in common. For example:

Mayumi can read music, and so can I.
Mayumi can't play chess, and neither can I.

Long and short forms of verbs

1 In this unit, you will practice some verbs that have a long form and a short form.

Long form written as:	Short form written as:	Short form pronounced as:
am	'm (I'm not ready.)	/m/
are	're (We're leaving now.)	/r/, /ər/
is	's (What's the matter?)	/s/, /z/, or /ɪz/
has	's (My mother's been there twice.)	/s/, /z/, or /ɪz/
have	've (They've already eaten.)	/v/, /əv/, or /ə/
had	'd (I asked if he'd seen it.)	/d/, /ɪd/
would	'd (She'd like to buy a car.)	/d/, /ɪd/
did	'd (Where'd they go?)	/d/, /ɪd/
will	'll (I think you'll like it.)	/l/, /əl/

 2 Short forms are used more in speaking than in writing, but they are often used in writing that shows conversation. Listen to this conversation. Write what you hear in the spaces. Use short forms when you hear them.

A: _____ like some of those apples.
How much _____?

B: _____ forty cents each. How
many _____ like?

A: _____ take five.

B: There _____. _____ like a
bag for them?

A: Yes, _____. _____ full.

B: Anything else?

A: No, _____ all, thanks. How much
_____?

B: _____ be two dollars.

A: _____ a twenty.

B: _____ got anything smaller?

A: Uh, _____ not sure. No, _____ all _____ got.

3 Listen again. Repeat the conversation one sentence at a time. Then work in pairs and say the conversation together. Don't forget to use *short* forms where you have written them.

4 Based on the examples in the conversation in **2**, complete the rules below. Choose from the words in the box on the right.

1. The _____ form of these verbs is used when the verb is the first or last word in a sentence.

2. The _____ form is often used in questions beginning with a question word (such as *how*) when another word (such as *much* or *many*) comes after the question word.

> short
> long

5 Look at this family and listen to the description.

Note that in speaking, short forms are used after both nouns and pronouns, but in writing, short forms are not common after nouns.

Judy
(born Jan. 3, 1963)

David
(born Feb. 16, 1962)

Hannah
(born Dec. 8, 1993)

Michael
(born Nov. 27, 1995)

Lawyer

Lawyer

Married 1992

Judy is 35 and David is 36. (Spoken: "Judy's thirty-five and David's thirty-six.")
They've been married for 6 years.
They're both lawyers.
They have two children.
Hannah is 4. She'll be 5 in December. (Spoken: "Hannah's four.")
Michael is 2. He'll be 3 in November. (Spoken: "Michael's two.")

Now describe the families on the next page aloud in the same way. Use the short forms of the verbs where possible.

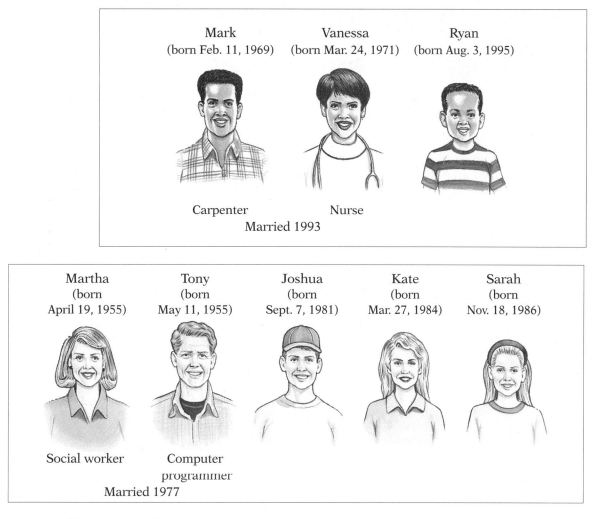

Mark
(born Feb. 11, 1969)

Vanessa
(born Mar. 24, 1971)

Ryan
(born Aug. 3, 1995)

Carpenter

Nurse

Married 1993

Martha
(born
April 19, 1955)

Tony
(born
May 11, 1955)

Joshua
(born
Sept. 7, 1981)

Kate
(born
Mar. 27, 1984)

Sarah
(born
Nov. 18, 1986)

Social worker

Computer
programmer

Married 1977

6 Work in pairs or small groups. Make *wrong* sentences about the families.

Listen to these examples.

A: Mark is 28. (Spoken: "Mark's twenty-eight.")
B: No, he isn't. He's 29.

A: Martha and Tony have been married for 18 years. (Spoken: "Martha and Tony've been . . .")
B: No, they haven't. They've been married for 21 years.

A: Hannah will be 4 in December. (Spoken: "Hannah'll be . . .")
B: No, she won't. She'll be 5.

Continue in the same way. Use the short form of the verbs where possible.

7 Look back at the sentences in **5**. If you have a brother, sister, or friend who has children, tell your partner or group about that person's family in the same way.

Weak forms of some pronouns; more on the long and short forms of verbs

1 In Unit 46, you practiced the weak form of *you*. Other pronouns have weak forms, too.

Listen and complete the sentences with words from the box.

he	him	she	her	it	they
them	you	your	my	we	

1. I lost _____ wallet.

2. _____ all would.

3. _____'s getting married.

4. _____'s ten to five.

5. Let's visit _____ sister.

6. I put _____ on the table.

7. _____'s five foot six.

8. Can't _____ take a cab?

9. I don't know. I haven't seen _____ lately.

10. I'll just tell _____ I already have plans.

11. I'm sorry. I tried to call _____ but _____ phone was busy.

2 Work in pairs. Match the answers in **1** with these questions.

a. What time is it? _4_

b. How tall is she? _____

c. What's the matter? _____

d. How's your brother? _____

e. Who'll drive them? _____

f. Where've you been? _____

g. Where are the tickets? _____

h. What's Eva been doing? _____

i. What'll you tell him? _____

j. Who'd like to come? _____

k. What would you like to do? _____

In Unit 47, you practiced the short form of verbs in statements. Notice that short forms can also be used in questions, especially when the verb comes directly after a question word (such as *what*, *who*, *where*, or *how*). Remember, though, that short forms are very common in spoken English, but they are used much less often in writing.

3 Repeat the conversations one line at a time and check your answers. Then say the conversations together with your partner.

4 Mrs. Valdez has two children. They went to play in the park but should have been home an hour ago. She is very worried and calls the police.

Listen to the conversation and decide which picture shows Chris and which shows Alex. (*Chris* and *Alex* can be either a girl's or a boy's name.) Write the names under the correct pictures.

a.   b.   c.   d.

5 Make as many short sentences as you can to describe Chris and Alex. Use the pictures to help you.

6 Choose a student in your class and describe him or her in the same way you have described Chris and Alex. Your classmates should try to guess who you are describing.

7 Listen to the strong form of these pronouns.

I   you   he   she   we   they

Repeat these pronouns with the short form of *will*. Notice that the vowel sound in the pronoun is more relaxed with the short form.

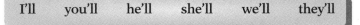

I'll   you'll   he'll   she'll   we'll   they'll

8 Work in small groups. Interview the other people in your group to find out what they think they'll be doing twenty years from now.

Ask questions like these. Add your own ideas. Do you think you'll . . .

be married?	own a house?	be rich?
be a parent?	own a car?	have your own business?
be a grandparent?	be famous?	be living in [the place you live now]?

9 Report your findings to the rest of the class. For example:

Sang-Moo thinks he'll be married. He'll have two children . . .

Weak forms of some conjunctions

 1 Which of the three words in the box do you hear in these sentences? Write one word in each space.

> and   or   but

1. a. Milk _____ no sugar.
   b. Milk _____ no sugar.

2. a. July _____ August.
   b. July _____ August.

3. a. It was small _____ very heavy.
   b. It was small _____ very heavy.

4. a. Amy _____ her friend.
   b. Amy _____ her friend.

5. a. _____ I want to go.
   b. _____ I want to go.

6. a. Red _____ green.
   b. Red _____ green.

 2 Listen again. Repeat the sentences and check your answers. Notice that the words in the spaces are pronounced with their *weak* forms.

3 Work with a partner. Say a sentence from each pair in **1**. Your partner should decide which of the sentences you are saying and should answer "b" or "a." Make sure that you use the weak form of the words in the spaces.

Take turns saying the sentences and answering.

4 Here are two more words that are usually used with their weak forms.

> as   than

 Look at the information on the map. Listen to these sentences and try to decide if they are true (*T*) or false (*F*). Notice the weak forms of *as* and *than*. Write *T* or *F* in the spaces.

1. _____ 2. _____ 3. _____ 4. _____ 5. _____ 6. _____ 7. _____ 8. _____

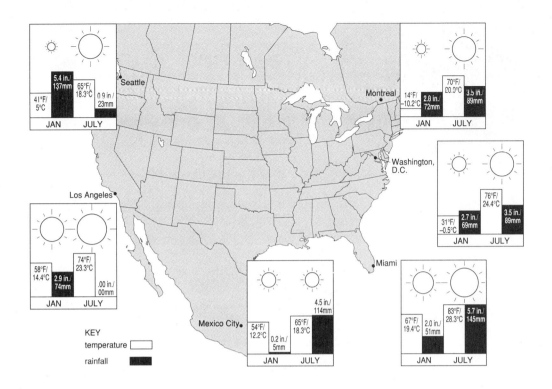

5 Work in pairs. Make sentences about the information on the map. Some should be true and some false. Say your sentences to the class. Your classmates should decide if your sentences are true or false.

Here is some language to help you. (Remember to use the weak forms of *as* and *than*.)

In January, July,	Mexico City Miami Seattle Washington Los Angeles Montreal	is	colder hotter warmer sunnier drier wetter	than	Montreal. Washington. ... ...

In January, July,	Mexico City Los Angeles Seattle Washington Montreal Miami	is (about)	as	cold hot sunny dry wet the same temperature as	as	Seattle. Miami. ... ...

Weak and strong forms of some prepositions

1 Look at these sentences. Decide which of these prepositions can fit in each space.

> at   for   from   of   to

Write your answers in the spaces on the right.

1. He was looking _____ the children in the park.   ___*for*___ / ___*at*___
2. I was home _____ six o'clock.   _____ / _____
3. They drove _____ Portland last night.   _____ / _____
4. He had a drawing _____ Rome.   _____ / _____
5. She picked up the ball and threw it _____ her brother.   _____ / _____
6. Do you like this picture? It's a present _____ Sarah.   _____ / _____
7. The people _____ France drink a lot of wine.   _____ / _____
8. She pointed _____ the ship.   _____ / _____

2 Now listen to the sentences. For each sentence, write the word you hear in the space.

3 Look at this table. All these prepositions have at least two pronunciations – a *strong form* and a *weak form*.

Listen and repeat the prepositions. First repeat the strong form, and then repeat the sentence or phrase with the weak form.

	Strong form	Weak form	
at	/æt/	/ət/	Look at this.
for	/fɔr/	/fər/	for you
from	/frəm/ or /frɑm/	/frəm/	from New York
to	/tuw/	/tə/	to New York
of	/əv/ or /ɑv/	/əv/ or /ə/	a pound of apples; a can of soup

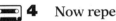 **4** Now repeat the sentences in **1**. Use the weak forms of the prepositions.

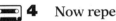 **5** Listen to these sentences. Write *S* in the space if you hear the *strong* form of the preposition and *W* if you hear the *weak* form.

1. What are you looking at? _____
2. I'm going to the post office. _____
3. Is it made of plastic? _____
4. I wonder where she's from. _____
5. What do you want it for? _____

6. Do you have change for a dollar? _____
7. It's not to Bill; it's from Bill. _____
8. What's it made of? _____
9. Let's meet at three. _____
10. Who are you writing to? _____

When are the *strong* forms of the prepositions used?

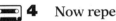 **6** Listen again and repeat the sentences.

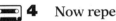 **7** Listen to this person talking about her plans for a trip around the eastern part of the United States. Follow the route she plans to take on the map.

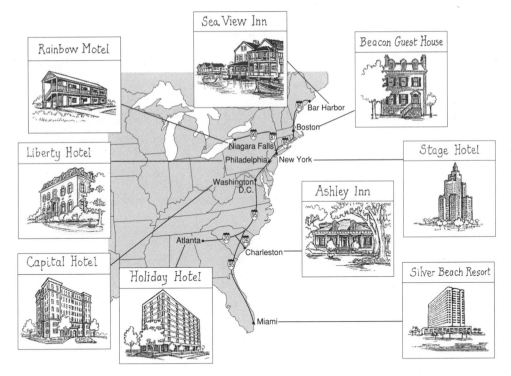

8 Plan *your* vacation using the same map and then tell your partner about it. You would like to see as much as possible, but you only have 12 days. You need to plan your trip carefully — the route, where you are going to stay, and how long you will stay in each place. Keep in mind that distances between places are often long (for example, Boston is about 1,570 miles [2,512 km] from Miami). Remember to use the weak forms of the prepositions *at, for, from, of,* and *to*.

Pronouncing -ed endings

1 Last week, Jane Garfield saw an accident from her office window. Later she told a friend about what she saw.

Listen to the conversation. As you listen, decide which of these headlines appeared in the local newspaper the day after the accident.

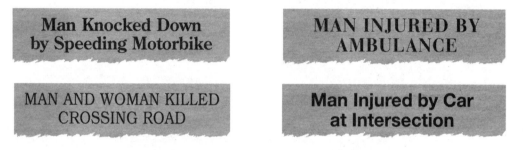

Man Knocked Down by Speeding Motorbike

MAN INJURED BY AMBULANCE

MAN AND WOMAN KILLED CROSSING ROAD

Man Injured by Car at Intersection

2 Repeat these words from the conversation you just heard.

walked	knocked	jumped	wanted	looked
explained	arrested	stopped	called	arrived
started	helped	carried	missed	

3 The *-ed* ending is pronounced in one of three ways. Listen again to the past tense *-ed* words from the story and write them in the table according to the pronunciation of the *-ed* ending.

/t/	/d/	/ɪd/
walked		

4 The pronunciation of *-ed* depends on the sound that comes before it. This table shows the sounds that come before *-ed* in the verbs in **3** when *-ed* is pronounced these three ways:

/t/	/d/	/ɪd/
/k/	/n/	/t/
/p/	/l/	
/s/	/v/	
	vowel sound	

5 Listen to the conversation again, and then try to retell the story.

If you need help, look at the sentences below and the words in the box in 2. The missing words are all past tense *-ed* verbs.

Jane Garfield was working in her office.

She ______________ to see what the weather was like.

She ______________ to the window and ______________ outside.

A car ______________ at the intersection.

A man and a woman ______________ to cross the road.

Another car drove through the intersection.

The woman ______________ out of the way.

The car just ______________ her.

It ______________ down the man.

Jane ______________ for an ambulance and the police.

They ______________ quickly.

The ambulance workers ______________ the woman to stand up.

They ______________ the man into the ambulance.

Jane ______________ what she had seen.

Later, the police ______________ the driver.

6 **Have you ever seen an accident or been involved in one? Tell your partner or the class about it. Pay particular attention to the pronunciation of past tense *-ed* endings.**

7 Work in pairs. Choose words from the box to complete these conversations. All the words end in *-ed*.

> laughed   walked   rained   arrived   finished   decided
> dropped   washed   passed   polluted   mailed

1. A: How was the weather?
   B: It _____ all the time.

2. A: How did the glass break?
   B: I _____ it.

3. A: Why didn't you go swimming?
   B: The water was _____.

4. A: Your check hasn't _____ yet.
   B: But I _____ it on Tuesday.

5. A: When can I see the painting?
   B: Not till I've _____ it.

6. A: How did your driving test go?
   B: I _____!

7. A: Was the movie funny?
   B: Yes, I _____ the whole time.

8. A: Which one are you going to buy?
   B: I haven't _____.

9. A: This floor is dirty.
   B: But I _____ it yesterday.

10. A: You look tired.
    B: I _____ all the way.

8 Repeat the conversations one line at a time and check your answers.

9 Using the *-ed* verbs in **7**, add sounds to the table in **4**.

10 Work in pairs. Tell a story to the rest of the class based on one of the pairs of pictures. They show the beginning and end of a story. The first sentence is given for each. Make notes and try to include as many past tense verbs ending in *-ed* as you can. Some notes for the first set of pictures are given as an example.

One day Daniel woke up, <u>looked</u> at the clock, and <u>realized</u> that he was late for work. . . .

Daniel woke up — <u>looked</u> at clock, <u>realized</u> late. <u>Washed</u>, shaved, and brushed teeth. <u>Hurried</u> downstairs. <u>Skipped</u> breakfast. <u>Walked</u> to bus stop. <u>Waited</u> 5 minutes until bus <u>arrived</u>. Got to office, <u>discovered</u> closed. Suddenly <u>remembered</u> it was Sunday!

The phone rang, and Elena <u>answered</u> it. . . .

The burglar <u>opened</u> the window quietly. . . .

11 Listen to the first story in **10**.

Unit 52 Pronouncing -s endings

1 The *-s* ending is pronounced as /s/, /z/, or /ɪz/. **Repeat these example words:**

1. Words that end with /s/: cats, keeps, takes, Beth's
2. Words that end with /z/: calls, gloves, toys, she's
3. Words that end with /ɪz/: catches, passes, boxes, Mitch's

The pronunciation used depends on the sound that comes before the final *-s* or *-es*.

Notice that *-s* endings include noun plurals (for example, *two cats*), third person singular verbs (*He takes the train*), possessives (*Beth's house*), and the short form of *is* or *has* (*What's her name? He's already left.*). They all follow the same pronunciation rules.

2 Listen to these groups of words. In each group, all the words except one have the same pronunciation at the end. Underline the odd one out in each group.

Remember to focus on the *sound* of the *-s* ending, not the spelling.

1. looks, sleeps, <u>runs</u>, cuts, hopes
2. finishes, <u>includes</u>, chooses, misses, watches
3. loses, calls, gives, sings, buys
4. plays, goes, rains, wears, gets
5. writes, laughs, speaks, touches, stops
6. begins, promises, drives, seems, sells
7. Jeff's, Bob's, David's, Jane's, Mary's

3 Listen again to the words in **2**, and repeat the words in each group. Decide which sounds are followed by the three sounds of the *-s* ending (/s/, /z/, and /ɪz/) and write them in the table.

/s/	/z/	/ɪz/
/k/ /p/	/n/ /d/ *vowel sound*	/ʃ/ (*spelled* <u>sh</u>)

When is *-es* pronounced as a separate syllable?

4 Work in pairs. Study these pictures for one minute. Then cover the pictures and try to remember what you saw. Your partner will check your answers. Concentrate on pronouncing the plural *s* correctly.

5 Look again at the things shown in the pictures in **4**. How is the plural *s* pronounced in each? If necessary, add more sounds to the table in **3**.

6 Find someone in your class who . . .

  1. likes old movies   _____

  2. enjoys telling jokes   _____

  3. wears contact lenses   _____

  4. reads history books for fun _____

  5. watches television less than two hours a week _____

  6. hates to shop for clothes   _____

  7. walks at least two miles every day _____

  8. loves animals   _____

  9. speaks three or more languages _____

10. plays sports every weekend _____

Ask questions like this:

  Do you like old movies?

Write the name of a person who answers "yes" in the space. Each name can be used only one time.

7 Report your answers to the rest of the class. For example:

  Ali likes old movies.

Concentrate on the correct pronunciation of the final *-s* or *-es*.

Letters and sounds

Written LETTERS stand for spoken SOUNDS. In some words, each letter stands for one sound – for example, in the word *dog* /dɔg/. In other words, there are more letters than sounds – for example, in the word *luck* /lək/. And sometimes, there are more sounds than letters – for example, in the word *box* /bɑks/.

1 Work in pairs. Decide whether the number of letters and sounds in these words is the same (S) or different (D). Put a check in the correct box.

	S	D		S	D		S	D
dog	☑	☐	window	☐	☐	not	☐	☐
luck	☐	☑	she	☐	☐	thin	☐	☐
cough	☐	☐	chess	☐	☐	mix	☐	☐
cats	☐	☐	bill	☐	☐	other	☐	☐
plan	☐	☐	most	☐	☐	young	☐	☐

 2 Repeat the words and check your answers.

3 Study the words in the box and decide how many ways the CONSONANT LETTERS can be pronounced. Write *1* in the space next to the consonant if it is pronounced only one way, and *2* if it is pronounced two ways.

keep	five	win	ahead	moon	book	age	take	red
car	double	swim	hat	leaf	police	green	visit	

b _____   g _____   m _____   s _____

c _____   h _____   n _____   t _____

d _____   k _____   p _____   v _____

f _____   l _____   r _____   w _____

Most single consonant letters have only one pronunciation. What consonant letters have you found that have *two* common pronunciations?

4   Look at this word chain.

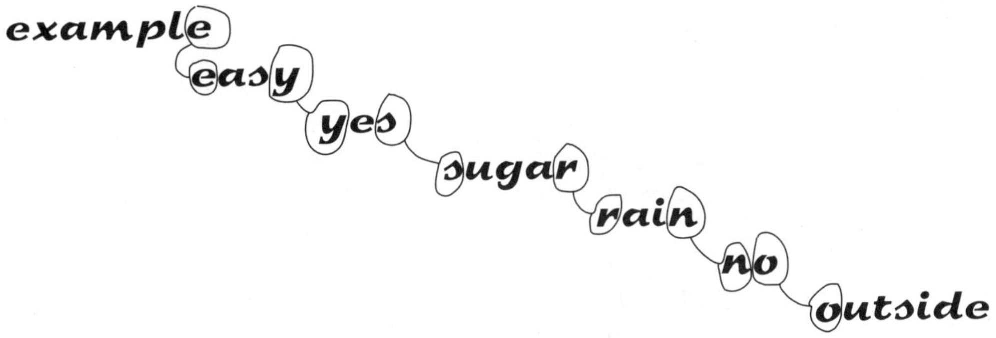

example
easy
yes
sugar
rain
no
outside

The first letter of each word is the same as the last letter of the previous word. Go around the class and make similar word chains. If you give a wrong word or can't think of a new word, you are out of the chain. Don't repeat a word in a chain. Remember to think about how words are spelled, not how they are pronounced.

Pronouncing consonant letters: c and g

1 In columns A and B, underline all the letter *c*'s that are pronounced /s/ (as in *sit*), and circle all the *c*'s that are pronounced /k/ (as in *cat*).

A

The traffi(c) is bad

I had a cup of coffee

I've been to

Only take this medicine

I went across the street

I can't decide

I haven't had a cigarette

Call

B

South Ameri(c)a twice.

what courses to take.

the police!

in the center of the city.

in an emergency.

since December.

at a cafe.

to the post office.

2 Work in pairs. Match the sentence halves in columns A and B.

3 Repeat the sentences and check your answers.

4 Complete this rule to tell you when to pronounce the letter *c* as /s/ (*sit*) and when to pronounce it as /k/ (*cat*).

The letter *c* is pronounced /s/ before the letters _____, _____, or _____ in a word, and it is pronounced /k/ everywhere else.

5 The rule for pronouncing the letter *g* is similar to the rule for pronouncing *c*. It is pronounced /dʒ/ (as in *page*) before the letters *e*, *i*, and *y*, and it is pronounced /g/ (as in *go*) everywhere else. But there are some common exceptions to this rule. Work in pairs. Underline the words in the box that break the rule.

good-bye	together	grandparents	stranger	bag	girl
cigarette	magic	dangerous	again	begin	Egypt
grass	give	engine	change	get	large	language
register	vegetables	Germany	forget

6 Repeat the words and check your answers.

7 Write one sentence that includes two or more words that have the letter *g*. Use the words in **5** or others you can think of. For example:

My g̲randparents went to G̲ermany in Au̲g̲ust.

Show your sentence to other members of the class and ask them to read it aloud. Check that they pronounce the letter *g* correctly.

Pronouncing *th*

1 The consonant pair *th* can have two pronunciations: /θ/ (*think*) and /ð/ (*these*). The words with *th* in the sentences on the left have the sound /ð/ (*these*). The words in the sentences on the right have the sound /θ/ (*think*).

Match these questions and answers.

How many are there?	Through here.
What's the matter?	On Thursday.
Is this yours?	I'm thirsty.
What time is their train?	A thousand.
Where are they?	No, he's thinner.
Is he heavier than me?	Three thirty.
What day will you be there?	Yes. Thank you.

2 Listen and check your answers.

3 Listen again. Repeat the conversations one line at a time. Then work in pairs and say the conversations together.

4 Look again at the words with *th* in **1**. Then complete the rule with the symbols in the box on the right.

At the beginning of a word, *th* is normally pronounced /___ / in grammar words (such as *the, they, them, that,* and *there*) and /___ / in other kinds of words.

> /θ/ (think)
> /ð/ (these)

5 Work in pairs. Say these words to your partner, and then complete the rule.

> mouth   birth   fourth   path   truth
> fifth   worth   month   north

When *th* is at the end of a word, it is usually pronounced /___ /.

6 The consonant pair *th* is in the middle of these words. Work in pairs and underline the words in which *th* is pronounced /ð/.

> father   bathroom   nothing   other   weather   birthday
> something   together   authority   either   rather   healthy

What do you notice about the endings of the words you have underlined? Complete this sentence to give you a simple rule about the pronunciation of *th* in the middle of words.

In the middle of a word, *th* is usually pronounced /ð/ if the word ends in _____.

 7 Repeat the words in the boxes in **5** and **6**.

8 Work in groups of three or four. Try to match the dates and the events. Say the dates like this: "July thirteenth, nineteen thirty" (July 13, 1930).

Joseph Stalin died.

Bill Clinton became President of the United States.

The first soccer World Cup was played in Uruguay.

> July 13, 1930   March 5, 1953   December 17, 1903
> June 30, 1997   January 20, 1993   April 6, 1896

Hong Kong was returned to China.

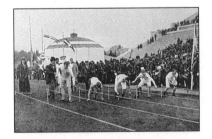
The first modern Olympic Games began in Athens, Greece.

The Wright brothers flew the first airplane.

9 Compare answers with the rest of the class.

Pronouncing *sh*, *ch*, and *gh*; other spellings for /ʃ/ and /tʃ/

1 Work in pairs. Study the words in the box and answer the questions.

shoes	washing machine	night	shampoo	Chinese
tough	ship	high	toothbrush	cheese	rough
sharp	ghost	shiver	chest	fish	shirt	stomach
cough	fresh	laugh	French	dishwasher	

1. How many ways are there of pronouncing *sh*? _____
2. The consonant pair *ch* is usually pronounced /tʃ/ (as in *cheese*). Find two words in which it is pronounced differently. _____ and _____
3. Find a word in which *gh* is pronounced /f/. _____
4. Find a word in which *gh* is not pronounced at all. _____
5. Find a word in which *gh* is pronounced a different way. _____

2 Repeat the words and check your answers.

3 Work in pairs. In the box in **1**, find *two* . . .

1. things you can eat	___*cheese*___	and _____
2. things you can wear	_____	and _____
3. things you can find in a bathroom	_____	and _____
4. things that use electricity	_____	and _____
5. things you do when you are sick	_____	and _____
6. parts of the body	_____	and _____
7. things you can see at sea	_____	and _____
8. languages	_____	and _____
9. words that can describe food	_____	and _____
10. words that can describe how something feels when you touch it	_____	and _____

4 Compare answers with the rest of the class.

5 Work in pairs. Write sentences for A to make short conversations. Then say the conversations together for the rest of the class.

1. A: _____
   B: When I'm finished washing the dishes.

2. A: _____
   B: She wrote a check.

3. A: _____
   B: I didn't have enough change.

4. A: _____
   B: I bought some shoes.

5. A: _____
   B: I didn't eat much for lunch.

6 The most common spelling for /ʃ/ (as in *shoe*) is *sh*, and the most common spelling for /tʃ/ (as in *cheese*) is *ch*. However, these sounds sometimes have different spellings, especially in words with some common endings.

Listen to these words and decide how the underlined letters are pronounced. Put a check in the correct box.

	/ʃ/	/tʃ/			/ʃ/	/tʃ/
1. information	☑	❏		9. special	❏	❏
2. furniture	❏	❏		10. commercial	❏	❏
3. education	❏	❏		11. temperature	❏	❏
4. tissue	❏	❏		12. examination	❏	❏
5. suggestion	❏	❏		13. natural	❏	❏
6. profession	❏	❏		14. delicious	❏	❏
7. question	❏	❏		15. national	❏	❏
8. musician	❏	❏		16. actual	❏	❏

7 Listen again. Repeat the words and check your answers.

8 Work in pairs. Try to decide how the underlined letters are pronounced in these words. Put a check in the correct box.

	/ʃ/	/tʃ/			/ʃ/	/tʃ/
1. future	❏	❏		4. official	❏	❏
2. discussion	❏	❏		5. position	❏	❏
3. conversation	❏	❏		6. picture	❏	❏

9 Repeat the words and check your answers.

Pronunciation, spelling, and word stress

📼 **1**   Listen to these words. How are the underlined letters pronounced?

along   collect   Canada   telephone

This sound is /ə/, called *schwa*.

2   Work in pairs. For each word in the box:

1. Draw a large circle over the stressed syllable.
2. Underline the letter or letters pronounced /ə/.

> across   problem   magazine   tomorrow   probably   profession
>
> curious   instrument   suggest   animal   common   committee

📼 **3**   Repeat the words and check your answers.

4   The stressed vowel /ə/ is usually spelled with the letters *u* (*bus*) or *o* (*come*), but the *unstressed* vowel /ə/ has many different spellings in English.

Look at the words in the box in **2**. How many ways have you found of spelling the unstressed /ə/ sound? Write them in the table.

Spelling	Example
a	*across*

📼 **5**   Repeat the words in the box on the next page. Underline the letters that are pronounced as unstressed /ər/.

Remember that when /r/ comes after /ə/, it changes the way /ə/ sounds.

daughter	doctor	percent	pleasure	regular	yesterday
neighbor	forward	forgot	modern	information	

What spellings have you found for /ər/? Write them in the space.

er, _____

6 Complete the sentence with a word from the box on the right.

Schwa is the most common vowel sound in _____ syllables.

stressed
unstressed

7 Work in pairs. Look at this picture and find as many things as you can that have the *unstressed* sound /ə/ (or /ər/) in their pronunciation. Write the words in the spaces and underline the /ə/ sounds.

pedestrian _____
movie theater _____
_____
_____
_____
_____
_____
_____
_____
_____
_____
_____
_____
_____
_____
_____
_____
_____
_____

Pronouncing single vowel letters

1 Repeat the names of these vowel letters.

a   e   i   o   u

2 Work in pairs. Say these abbreviations.

USA   UN   CEO   VIP   CIA   UFO   IOU   ESL

What do they stand for?

3 All the words in the box have one syllable with one vowel letter in the middle. Underline all the words that have a vowel that is pronounced with its NAME SOUND (or, in the case of *u*, with the sound /uw/, as in *too*).

cake	fact	life	tap	cup	left	home
these	bit	cute	spell	bag	drop	
tape	smile	rule	soft	nose	kill	dust

4 Repeat the words in the box in **3** and check your answers.

5 In the table, C stands for a consonant letter, V stands for a vowel letter, and e is the letter *e*. (C) stands for a *possible* consonant letter. For example, -VC(C) could be -VC (as in *ten*) or -VCC (as in *send* or *clock*). Only the last part of the word is shown, from the vowel until the end, since this is the part of the word that is important for deciding how to pronounce the vowel.

In each word in the box in **3**, look at the vowel in the middle and the letters that come *after* it. Write the word in the correct column in the table.

Vowel	-VCe	-VC(C)
a	*cake*	
e		
i		
o		
u		

6 Complete the sentence to make a rule about how to pronounce the vowel letters in most one-syllable words.

When the written form of a one-syllable word ends with _____, the first vowel letter is usually pronounced with its name.

There are some common exceptions to this rule. For example, the vowels in *give*, *love*, and *have* are not pronounced with their names. There is a rule in English that words cannot end with the letter *v*, so all words with *v* at the end add a final *e*.

7 Repeat these words.

map   best   fish   hot   fun

The vowel sound in each of these words is sometimes called the BASE SOUND of the vowel.

8 Look at the words in the table in **5** and complete the sentence to make another rule about how to pronounce the vowel in one-syllable words. Fill in the spaces with the correct spelling patterns from the box on the right.

When the written form of a one-syllable word ends with _____ or _____, the vowel letter is usually pronounced with its base sound.

> VC
> VCe
> VCC

Again, there are exceptions to the rule. For example, vowels before the consonants *l* and *r* are usually pronounced differently (as in the words *call*, *car*, *bird*, and *short*). And some speakers pronounce many words spelled with -oCC (for example, *soft*, *lost*, and *across*) with the vowel sound /ɔ/.

9 The rules for pronouncing vowels in words that have more than one syllable are complicated, but there are a few simple rules that can help.

The two rules you learned for one-syllable words also usually work for the *last* syllable of longer words if the syllable is *stressed*. Remember that the most common vowel sound in *unstressed* syllables is schwa (/ə/).

Using these rules, look at the following words. Work in pairs. Put a circle over the stressed syllable. Then look at the vowel in the last syllable and try to decide how it is pronounced – with its name sound (*N*), with its base sound (*B*), or as schwa (*S*). Write *N*, *B*, or *S* in the space.

1. minute   *S*   3. purpose _____   5. interrupt _____

2. suppose *N*   4. confuse _____   6. assistant _____

7. private _____   10. encourage _____   13. determine _____

8. accurate _____   11. represent _____   14. define _____

9. relate _____   12. frequent _____

10   Repeat the words and check your answers.

11   The rule for pronouncing the vowel in the spelling -VCC applies to *any* stressed syllable. The words in the box all have stress on the first syllable. Which vowel sound would you use in the first syllable, the name sound or the base sound?

1	2
nickel	Russia
doctor	slippers
Moscow	rubber
summer	hospital
sandals	dollar
broccoli	package
letter	winter
plastic	cabbage

12   Work in pairs. Look at the words in the box in **11**. Make connections between the words in column 1 and the words in column 2. For example:

There are twenty nickels in a dollar.

13   Report your answers to the rest of the class.

Unit 59 — Pronouncing vowel pairs

In Unit 59, you will learn about the pronunciation of two vowel letters together (a VOWEL PAIR). Many vowel pairs can be pronounced in more than one way. For example:

> The vowel pair *oa* is pronounced /ow/ in *boat* and /ɔ/ in *broad*.
> The vowel pair *ei* is pronounced /iy/ in *receive* and /ey/ in *eight*.

Often, one pronunciation is much more common than another. For example, the vowel pair *oa* is usually pronounced /ow/ (*boat*) rather than /ɔ/ (*broad*). The vowel pair *ei* is usually pronounced /iy/ (*receive*), though it often has the sound /ey/ (*eight*) before the letters *g* or *n*.

1 Work in pairs. What are the missing letters? Complete each word with one of these vowel pairs.

ee
oo
ea

1. thr_____
2. sp_____n
3. w_____l
4. cl_____n
5. betw_____n
6. ch_____p
7. aftern_____n
8. c_____king
9. eight_____n
10. sl_____p
11. _____sy
12. h_____vy
13. sch_____l
14. _____t
15. alr_____dy
16. br_____k

2 Repeat the words and check your answers.

3 Write each of the words from **1** in the correct box in the table, according to the vowel pair found in each word and the way this vowel pair is pronounced. Some of the boxes in the table will remain empty.

	/iy/ (piece)	/ey/ (day)	/uw/ (June)	/ɛ/ (red)	/ʊ/ (put)
ee					
oo			spoon		
ea					

4 Listen to this conversation and then write words from the box in the spaces. All the words contain the vowel pair *ou*.

trouble	out	south	fabulous	blouse	cousin	serious
you	group	cloudy	sounds	would	mountains	
dangerous	country	souvenirs	house	tourists	found	

A: How was your vacation?

B: _____!

A: You went to Colorado, right?

B: Right.

A: Did a _____ of _____ go?

B: No, just my _____ and me.

A: Where did you stay? Did you camp _____?

B: No, actually, we rented a _____ in Boulder.

A: Wow, it _____ great!

B: Yeah. The _____ around there was beautiful.

A: How was the weather?

B: Well, kind of _____.

A: What did you do there? Did you do any shopping?

B: Oh, I bought some _____. And I _____ this _____.

A: It's nice. What else did you do?

B: We went _____ for a few days for some skiing in the _____.

A: I've never gone skiing. It sounds too _____.

B: Well, I've had a few falls, but nothing too _____.

A: _____ you go back?

B: I'd like to. The only _____ was, there were too many _____!

5 Repeat the words in the box in **4**. Then work in pairs and say the conversation together.

6 The vowel pair *ou* is pronounced in five different ways in the words in the box in **4**. Group them and write them here.

1. *fabulous,* _____

2. *country,* _____

3. *group,* _____

4. *house,* _____

5. *tourists,* _____

Which group do you think shows the most common pronunciation for *ou*?

7 Work in small groups. Discuss what kind of vacation you prefer. Use some of these questions, but think of others if you can.

Do you prefer . . .

to stay in your own country or travel to another country?
to travel by boat or by train?
to sleep late or get up early?
to stay in one place or to travel around and see lots of places?
to eat out all the time or to cook meals yourself?

Do you prefer staying in a place . . .

near mountains or near the coast?
with dry but cool weather or hot but humid (wet) weather?
with a swimming pool or near a beach?

Unit 60   Silent letters

1 Many words contain letters that are not pronounced.

 Listen to these words and draw a line through the letter in each word that is not pronounced.

> raspberry   climb   knee   island   half
> column   know   handkerchief   listen   knife
> hour   two   Christmas   answer   vegetable
> comb   honest   talk   handsome   sign
> psychology   every   business   calm*

*Some Americans and Canadians pronounce all the letters in this word.

2 Listen again and repeat the words.

3 Work in pairs. Decide whether the underlined letter in each word is silent. How many words in each line have a silent letter? Write the number in the space.

1. milk, could, walk, build, cold _____
2. honor, oh, exhausted, hotel, rhythm _____
3. doubt, bulb, lamb, remember, bomb _____
4. foreign, ignore, signature, designer, resign _____
5. candle, Wednesday, midnight, window, couldn't _____

4 Listen and check your answers.

5 Some other words contain letters that may be pronounced when the word is said slowly and carefully, but are not normally pronounced when the word is said in conversation.

Listen and repeat. These words are said twice: first, slowly and carefully, and then at normal speed. *Listen* to the words said slowly, and *repeat* the words said at normal speed.

interesting   chocolate   practically   government   elementary
several   average   postcard   different   family   factory
valuable   comfortable   aspirin   grandfather   favorite

6 Draw a line through the letter in each word that is not pronounced when the word is said at normal speed.

 7 Repeat the sentences on the right. They all include a word from the box in **5**.

What's for dessert?	The government's raising taxes.
How often do you play softball?	No, they're different.
What's on the news?	Chocolate cake.
My car was broken into.	She just started elementary school.
Do you like this chair?	Several times.
How's your report going?	Was anything valuable taken?
What's your daughter doing?	Twice a week on the average.
What do you think of this color?	The other one's more comfortable.
Are these jackets the same?	It's practically finished.
Have you ever been to Montreal?	It's my favorite.

8 Match the sentences on the left with the sentences on the right. Then work in pairs and say the conversations together.

9 Work in pairs to write conversations similar to those in **7**. Use the words given.

1. book
   interesting

2. mail
   postcard

3. weekend
   family

4. headache
   aspirin

5. picture
   grandfather

6. work
   factory

1. A: What's the book like?
B: It's really interesting.

Then say the conversations you have written to the rest of the class.

Acknowledgments

Illustrations

Keith Bendis   1 *(top)*, 2, 3, 9, 14, 27, 43, 58, 70, 74, 83, 88, 108, 113, 137, 145
Daisy de Puthod   26, 28, 30, 45, 121, 140
Wally Neibart   4, 5, 21, 24, 41, 67, 78, 127
Kevin Spaulding   1 *(bottom)*, 19, 20, 25, 32 *(middle)*, 35 *(top)*, 56, 68, 86, 96, 114, 115
Andrew Toos   6, 7, 11, 17, 31, 32 *(top and bottom)*, 37, 38, 47, 48, 62, 63, 72, 81, 91, 101, 117, 124, 125, 142

Photographs

12   *(top and bottom)* © Roy Morsch/The Stock Market, © Ed Bock/The Stock Market, © Peter Beck/The Stock Market

55   *(top row, left to right)* © Roberto Arakaki/International Stock, © Tibor Bognár/The Stock Market, © Hiroshi Harada/Photo Researchers; *(bottom row, left to right)* © G. Anderson/The Stock Market, © ZEFA/The Stock Market, © Robert Frerck/Woodfin Camp & Associates

133   *(top row, left to right)* © Hulton Getty Picture Collection/Tony Stone Images, © Uniphoto Picture Agency, © Popperfoto/Archive Photos; *(bottom row, left to right)* © Harvey Lloyd/The Stock Market, © Popperfoto/Archive Photos, © Corbis-Bettmann